Cambridge Elements

Elements in Women Theatre Makers
edited by
Elaine Aston
Lancaster University
Melissa Sihra
Trinity College Dublin

CHINESE FEMINISMS AND *THE VAGINA MONOLOGUES*

Yingjun Wei
Trinity College Dublin

Shaftesbury Road, Cambridge CB2 8EA, United Kingdom

One Liberty Plaza, 20th Floor, New York, NY 10006, USA

477 Williamstown Road, Port Melbourne, VIC 3207, Australia

314–321, 3rd Floor, Plot 3, Splendor Forum, Jasola District Centre, New Delhi – 110025, India

103 Penang Road, #05–06/07, Visioncrest Commercial, Singapore 238467

Cambridge University Press is part of Cambridge University Press & Assessment, a department of the University of Cambridge.

We share the University's mission to contribute to society through the pursuit of education, learning and research at the highest international levels of excellence.

www.cambridge.org
Information on this title: www.cambridge.org/9781009667777
DOI: 10.1017/9781009667821

© Yingjun Wei 2026

This publication is in copyright. Subject to statutory exception and to the provisions of relevant collective licensing agreements, no reproduction of any part may take place without the written permission of Cambridge University Press & Assessment.

When citing this work, please include a reference to the DOI 10.1017/9781009667821

First published 2026

A catalogue record for this publication is available from the British Library

ISBN 978-1-009-66777-7 Hardback
ISBN 978-1-009-66779-1 Paperback
ISSN 2634-2391 (online)
ISSN 2634-2383 (print)

Cambridge University Press & Assessment has no responsibility for the persistence or accuracy of URLs for external or third-party internet websites referred to in this publication and does not guarantee that any content on such websites is, or will remain, accurate or appropriate.

For EU product safety concerns, contact us at Calle de José Abascal, 56, 1°, 28003 Madrid, Spain, or email eugpsr@cambridge.org

Chinese Feminisms and *The Vagina Monologues*

Elements in Women Theatre Makers

DOI: 10.1017/9781009667821
First published online: January 2026

Yingjun Wei
Trinity College Dublin
Author for correspondence: Yingjun Wei, weiyi@tcd.ie

Abstract: This Element focuses on three Chinese productions of *The Vagina Monologues* (*TVM*, 1996), a radical-feminist play by the North American artist and activist Eve Ensler: *Yin Dao Du Bai* (*The Vagina Monologues*, 2003), *Yin Dao Zhi Dao* (*Vagina's Way*, 2013), and *Dao Yin* (*Saying Vagina*, 2021). Each production was staged in and informed by the changing landscape of Chinese feminism: from 2003 to the early 2010s, the making of *TVM* was a process of exploring the subject position of an autonomous citizen, but from 2015, feminist theatre making had to contend with gains being eroded by state neo-liberalism, an issue reflected in the third performance, *Dao Yin* (2021). Drawing on this historical analysis, in the fifth and final section the Element proposes the concept of 'collapsed feminisms' to argue that Chinese feminist theatres from 2003 to 2021 staged an extremely complicated scene where all these feminisms overlapped and 'collapsed' together.

Keywords: *The Vagina Monologues*, feminist theatre, contemporary Chinese feminism, transnational feminism, theatre historiography

© Yingjun Wei 2026

ISBNs: 9781009667777 (HB), 9781009667791 (PB), 9781009667821 (OC)
ISSNs: 2634-2391 (online), 2634-2383 (print)

Contents

1 *The Vagina Monologues* and Feminism(s) in China   1

2 The Politics of Desire: Feminist Erotic Desires in *Yin Dao Du Bai* and (Neo-)Liberalism   12

3 *Vagina's Way*: Confronting Medical-Patriarchal-Nationalist Ideologies in and beyond Feminist Theatre   26

4 Feminist Theatre during the Covid-19 Pandemic: *Dao Yin* and Neo-liberal Globalization   39

5 Conclusion: Collapsed Feminisms, Chaos, Relics, and Feminist Hope   50

References   57

1 *The Vagina Monologues* and Feminism(s) in China

'The body is the scene.' This is a quotation from a feminist activist involved in the 'Nude Bodies for Anti-domestic Violence' petition in 2012 (Wang, 2019: 155),[1] – a performative intervention in which activists used their naked bodies and red paint to stage a spectacle on Weibo (a major Chinese social media platform) advocating for anti-domestic violence legislation. The notion of the 'body' as the 'scene' of activism gestures to embodiment and performativity as core to the practice of feminism. Through performative practices, contemporary feminists ask: what does it mean to be a female subject? What can be made of the subject matter of Chinese feminism? How can Chinese feminism be embodied and enacted?

These three fundamental questions, which, as I shall shortly explain, began to emerge in the early twentieth century, continue to resonate a century later. Inspired by the idea that 'the body is the scene', this Element explores these enduring questions by focusing on the theatre-making practices of contemporary Chinese feminists. More specifically, by analysing three Chinese adaptations of *The Vagina Monologues* (1996) – *Yin Dao Du Bai* (*The Vagina Monologues*, 2003), *Yin Dao Zhi Dao* (*Vagina's Way*, 2013), and *Dao Yin* (*Saying Vagina*, 2021) – it examines how, since the early twenty-first century, feminists have been repositioning themselves and reclaiming their subjectivity. These adaptations of North American playwright and activist Eve Ensler's radical-feminist play have both contributed to – and mirrored – the continuities of and radical ruptures in contemporary Chinese feminist movements. To set the contemporary feminist scene for these adaptations it is helpful to briefly trace the lineage of Chinese feminism.

1.1 Chinese Feminism from Ibsen's *A Doll's House* to Eve Ensler's *The Vagina Monologues*

In the 1920s, Nora, the heroine of Henrik Ibsen's *A Doll's House* (1879), became a powerful symbol of Chinese women's emancipation. As the play was introduced to China, its themes of individual freedom and female liberation resonated deeply, shaping feminist discourse at that time. In 1923, Chinese modernist literary pioneer Lu Xun delivered the public speech 'What Happens after Nora Walks Out', igniting fervent discussions amid a burgeoning feminist movement, core to which was women's emancipation. As Lu Xun argued, true liberation required more than simply leaving the household; it necessitated

---

[1] This quote comes from feminist activist Datu's Weibo post responding to misogynistic comments on radical-feminist art against domestic violence, which features female nudity. Datu writes: 'The body is the scene, why [are you] so scared and over reacting [*sic*]?' (cited in Di Wang, 2019, 155).

women's access to the public sphere, secured through economic rights and broader social transformation (Hu, 2023: 290). However, advocacy for women's emancipation from the family, Confucian traditions, and feudal codes of conduct – though directly addressing women's rights – was ultimately a secondary project within the larger pursuit of modernity. The movement for the 'new women (*xin nvxing*)' was largely driven by elite male intellectuals who prioritized the creation of a modern republic over gender equality. As theatre scholar Liyang Xia notes, 'Ibsen and his play *A Doll's House* have long held an important position in China's mainstream discourse on the nation's modernization process. In this discourse, the "new youth" – by and large male Ibsenites – take the foreground in Chinese women's emancipation movement' (2021: 218–219). Furthermore, Chinese feminism was promiscuously entangled with anti-colonialism, modernity, modernization, and nationalism. Emerging as a by-product of male political and cultural elites' response to colonialism and imperialism, modern Chinese feminism framed 'intimate bonding between women and state', refracting women's shared struggles against colonial oppression and aspirations for national liberation and modernization (Hu, 2020: 106).

Going into the 1930s, Maoist socialist feminism shaped feminist discourse in China by introducing 'class' as a key category, transforming Chinese women into socialist revolutionary subjects (*fünv*, meaning women) and loosening feminism's historical entanglement with colonial modernity (Barlow, 2004: 8, 38). However, this model adhered to a rigid, top-down approach to women's liberation, marked by inconsistency and vacillation due to the inherently patriarchal nature of hierarchical systems (Wang, 2005: 519–520). The All-China Women's Federation (ACWF) is emblematic of this feminist strand. Established in April 1949, and initially named the All-China Women's Democratic Federation, the ACWF was created as an umbrella organization for existing women's groups across the country, endorsed by the top leaders of the Chinese Communist Party (CCP) (521). Through its efforts, the ACWF has sought to transform women into 'statist subjects ... as a coherent part of the patriarchal state', advancing *funü gongzuo* (women-work) in alignment with the Party's central objectives. Since its inception, the ACWF has persistently addressed women's issues such as equal rights and welfare, mobilizing women to move beyond domestic households and participate actively in 'social production', 'civil administration', and 'public security' – integral components of China's modernization efforts (523, 529). Despite maintaining a certain degree of autonomy, the Federation remains largely aligned with the state's objectives. This alignment includes the state's disciplinary regulations relating to women's roles, viewing reproduction through marriage as a biopolitical tool for achieving state goals. This tension is epitomized by its endorsement of traditional gender roles, exemplified by the labelling of unmarried women aged above twenty-seven as 'leftover women' in 2007 (Fincher, 2014: 14; Liu, Huang, and Ma, 2015: 12). Moreover, its approach to feminist issues such as anti-domestic violence is often limited by the need to preserve the family institution, thereby ensuring that the modern Chinese family remains intact: 'the ACWF had earlier addressed the issue and had intervened to resolve conflicts within the family for many years, thus entering the private sphere of people's lives. However, the issue had not been considered a public and politically interesting matter' (Milwertz, 2003: 649).

It was only with the advent of China's transformation into a market economy and its turn towards a burgeoning neo-liberal ethos in the late 1970s that state-defined feminism gradually began to unravel as bottom-up feminist movements emerged, redirecting focus from class struggle to women's autonomy and self-organization. Facing 'a capital accumulation crisis in the 1970s and the 1980s', the party-state implemented neo-liberal reforms aimed at 'reinvent[ing]and liberat[ing] the market from the state' and 're-integrat[ing] China into the capitalist world economy in order to speed up capital accumulation' (So and Chu, 2012: 170). This approach, often termed *state neo-liberalism*, differs from the neo-liberalism practised in more advanced capitalist economies. It represents a paradoxical fusion: on the one hand are market-oriented policies such as 'decollectivisation', 'marketisation policy', 'fiscal decentralization and the weakening of the central state', and 'an open-door policy toward foreign investments'; on the other hand is continued strong state regulation, including tax mechanisms and 'redistribution' (170). By the late 1990s, as this state neo-liberal model reached maturity, a new 'fusion' had occurred: 'the emerging state-capitalist relationship' characterized by the interweaving of 'the political capital of the cadres, the economic capital of the capitalists, and the social and network capital embedded in the local society' (175).

The economic transition was also accompanied by a relatively relaxed yet equally paradoxical political climate, one oscillating between the will of the party-state and the expanding economic freedom. The transformation into a market economy, combined with a pervasive neo-liberal ethos marked by rising individualism and privatization within public culture, created the conditions for more autonomous feminist practices to emerge. The 1980s and 1990s saw the rise and growth of the non-governmental organization (NGO) path of Chinese feminism (Milwertz and Bu, 2007: 144). This movement peaked during the 1995 Fourth World Conference on Women (FWCW) in Beijing, which marked significant 'feminist conceptual, organizational, and social transformations in China' (Wang and Zhang, 2010: 40). In the wake of the FWCW, Chinese feminists engaged in a myriad of socio-cultural initiatives:

> They initiated programs to address a wide range of issues, such as domestic violence, gender and development, feminist curricular transformation in higher education, legal aid for women, rural women's political participation, sex-ratio imbalances, vocational training for rural women and unemployed urban women, and cultural productions that challenged sexist sexual norms, such as staging a Chinese version of *The Vagina Monologues*. (Wang, 2017: 169)

Where Ibsen's Nora 'characterized' Chinese feminism in the 1920s, *The Vagina Monologues* (*TVM*) appear in Chinese diasporic feminist scholar Wang Zheng's list of initiatives as a seminal exemplification of theatre operating as a site of counter-cultural, feminist resistance. That Wang specifies a 'Chinese version' of the play highlights the political and cultural potential of *localized* productions in the practice of Chinese feminism.

Over the past twenty years, *TVM* is the only Western women's play to achieve a significant and long-lasting impact in China, where it continues to remain relevant in and beyond the theatre. It is uniquely entangled with the evolution of Chinese feminism. In contrast to the influence of Ibsen's Nora, which was largely confined to a modernist discourse, *TVM* has been actively engaged by feminists and staged for specific feminist purposes. Both as a feminist play and as a catalyst for global grassroots campaigns, *TVM* is deeply interwoven with the history as well as the historiography of Chinese feminism, particularly given its wide-ranging social impact. Its methodology and socially engaged form, based on interviews and semi-verbatim theatre, make it especially adaptable to local contexts. The fact that each production of *TVM* studied in this Element has emerged at a crucial turning point in Chinese feminist politics, theory, and activism suggests that these productions are themselves valuable entry points into the historiography of Chinese feminism – something that cannot be said of any other contemporary women's theatre in China. Hence, my exclusive focus on *TVM*.

1.2 Young Feminist Activists

What the emergence of *TVM* in China also marks is the way in which feminists began to foreground their bodies as the primary medium of feminist expression. Such embodied practices are direct, extralinguistic, and unmediated, presenting a powerful contrast to the historically linguistic pathways – such as 'new women' and *fünv* – through which feminist identities had previously been constructed. Hence, although contemporary Chinese feminism carries the legacy of using theatre – such as the female heroine Nora – to contest gender norms, it significantly departs from earlier approaches predominantly shaped by male intellectual discourses on modernity. Instead, it emphasizes female and feminist autonomy, centring feminist subjects proposed and practised by women. In brief, this shift signifies a new era in Chinese feminism, where the corporeal presence of activists speaks volumes in a non-logocentric manner.

Post-1995 feminists have rejected the notion of a 'state patriarch' or 'socialist patriarch' as the 'champion' of women's liberation (Wang, 2005: 519–520). In the twenty-first century, particularly in the early 2010s, a new wave of grassroots feminists – referred to as 'Young Feminist Activists (YFAs)' (Liu, Huang, and Ma, 2015: 15) – emerged. Among them, theatre makers and activists involved in *TVM* productions and V-Day activism (a transnational feminist campaign against violence towards women inspired by Ensler's *TVM*) played a significant role. These activists sought to distance themselves from NGO feminism, turning away from what they termed 'embedded feminism', which they saw as remaining in a symbiotic relationship with the state (Li and Li, 2017: 4). Instead, they aligned themselves more closely with the global trend of youthful feminist activism, exemplified by movements such as Femen (Ukraine, 2008), Pussy Riot (Russia, 2011), and the Guerrilla Girls (US, 1985) (Rosenberg, 2016: 219–227). As Tiina Rosenberg observes, transnational feminist protest cultures have 'taken advantage of anarchist suspicions against capital and state' (223), and are 'radically individualistic' (224). The year 2012 saw several prominent feminist performances take place in both digital public spaces and the streets, including 'Occupy Men's Toilets' (2012), 'Toilet on Our Back' (2012), and 'Bloody Brides' (2012), among others. These performances advocated for gender equality and the improvement of women's rights and living conditions, each addressing a specific issue such as women's access to public infrastructure, anti-domestic violence, rural women's rights, LGBTQ rights, equal pay, and equal education for women. Although many of these YFAs operate independently, some have joined grassroots feminist networks, collaborating on these crucial issues. Unlike NGO feminism, these grassroots networks – such as Feminist Voices (*nüquan zhisheng*), BCome (see Section 3), and the Vagina Project (see Section 4) – exhibit greater flexibility in their organizing, as they remain unaffiliated with the state. They embody a rebellious spirit, are deeply interconnected with global movements, and possess a 'strong, independent sense of citizen subjectivity' (*qianglie de, duli de, gongmin zhutixing*).[2] For these activists, 'feminism is a plain fact of daily life' (Zheng, 2016: 38). Operating in a guerrilla-like fashion, they are pioneering new

---

[2] Comment by Ai Xiaoming, the convener and director of *Yin Dao Du Bai* (*The Vagina Monologues*, 2013). For more details, see Zhao, 2016.

avenues of resistance, employing theatre and performance as playful yet politically provocative tools to advance their feminist agenda in creatively expressive ways. 'Disorderly aesthetics' – 'feminist nudity' and 'home-made terminology of resistance, including vulgar words, humorous obscenities and *double-entendres*' – coined by Katrien Jacobs (2016: 822–823), for example, best characterizes Chinese performative feminism, particularly its political, affective, and performative dimensions. Beyond their non-state affiliation, YFAs often find their agendas at odds with state policies, particularly in their advocacy for LGBTQ rights. Although homosexuality was de-pathologized in China in 1989 (Wu, 2003: 128), LGBTQ individuals still lack legal and social recognition. The political risks of this divergence were made evident with the arrest of the 'Feminist Five' in 2015, leading YFAs to stage contemporary Chinese feminist performative acts.[3] This incident exposes the fraught relationship between feminist advocacy and state approval, revealing the precarious nature of pursuing gender equality and women's rights in a restrictive political environment.

Wang's inclusion of the Chinese *TVM* in broader post-1995 feminist endeavours inspires me to consider the three productions presented in this Element as both mirroring and responding to the shifting feminist climate. Together, *Yin Dao Du Bai*/*The Vagina Monologues*, 2003 (Section 2), *Yin Dao Zhi Dao*/ *Vagina's Way*, 2013 (Section 3), and *Dao Yin*/*Saying Vagina*, 2021 (Section 4) span pivotal paradigm shifts in Chinese feminisms. Specifically, from 2003 to the early 2010s, the making of *TVM* was a process of exploring the subject position of an autonomous citizen, but from 2015 onwards feminist theatre making had to contend with gains being eroded by state neo-liberalism, an issue reflected in the production of *Dao Yin*. Each production is presented and analysed within this adapting feminist culture, with analysis encompassing script, performance, organization, spectatorship, and funding. All three case studies treat theatre and performative activism as embodied mediums, whose aesthetic potential and political efficacy offer a unique entry point into Chinese feminist aesthetics, female bodily experiences and imaginaries, feminist compromises, and hopes.

1.3 A Transnational Feminist Framework

At the same time, this Element positions these Chinese productions within a transnational feminist framework, particularly in relation to Ensler's *TVM* and the global V-Day campaign. Since its premiere in October 1996 at the HERE Arts Center Off-Broadway, *TVM* has left an indelible mark on audiences

---
[3] See Section 4 for more detailed discussions on the arrest of the 'Feminist Five'.

across the United States and beyond, gaining international recognition since the late 1990s (Gallo-Cruz and Tulinski, 2020: 208). Beyond its chronological alignment with Chinese activists' shift towards a more autonomous approach, a key question arises: why has *TVM*, a late 1990s American dramatic work, remained a relevant reference for contemporary Chinese feminists? As its impact grew, critical voices from across the political spectrum emerged, fuelling controversy and cementing the play as a provocative cultural 'touchstone' (207). As noted by Alyssa Reiser, criticism comes from a broad spectrum: 'Right-wing Christians and other religious fundamentalists; the Intersex Society of North America; Betty Dodson; political conservatives; college administrations; mainstream theatre critics; feminist scholars and activists; founders of the Boston Women's Health Collective; and women living in the Global South have all spoken out against the Monologues' (2006: 3). Ensler's *TVM* draws notable parallels with the second-wave feminism of the 1960s and 1970s, positioning women's anatomy as a potent source of empowerment. This feminist wave foregrounded bodily autonomy and championed sexual freedom, frequently employing diverse artistic forms to elevate feminist consciousness. This chronological mismatch has drawn criticism from feminist scholars. Feminist sociologist Martha McCaughey argues that the play represents 'a reverse discourse' rather than 'a deconstructive one' as it frames women's bodies through a reductionist lens – one that risks objectifying them rather than empowering them as active agents (2013: 932). Elaine Aston notes that *TVM* features 'feminist sharing', a practice central to the advocacy style of 1970s feminism. She observes that while theatre was commonly used as 'a forum for sharing women's experience and knowledge' and was 'characteristic of much feminist theatre in the 1970s', it 'was far less common in the 1990s' (2003: 56–57). In a similarly incisive critique, Jill Dolan argues that '[*TVM*] seemed reminiscent of an earlier historical moment, of the consciousness-raising days, when we took that necessary first step of acknowledging ourselves as women and the personal nature of our politics. But after a decade of theorizing, practicing, and refining our politics, this reverential stance towards ourselves as women seems simplistic and conservative' (1998: 94).

The controversy surrounding the play and its chronological inappropriateness lies precisely in how female sexuality, particularly vaginal sexuality, should be positioned within feminism. The underlying body politics of *TVM* have often been criticized for their gender essentialism, as they equate vaginahood with womanhood. Susan E. Bell and Susan M. Reverby lament that Ensler 'undoes the very hard work of second-wave feminists who debunked the political, not just "pleasure", consequences of the myth of the vaginal orgasm' (2005: 434). Similarly, Aston contends that this approach to feminism 'risks an essentialist reduction of women to Woman/vagina' (2003: 56–57). While *TVM* echoes the second-wave ethos of interrogating female sexuality as a site of contestation, it paradoxically shifts the focus towards individual identity ('I') rather than feminist collective action. This post-feminist pursuit of self-actualization was also problematic for 'radical women of color' and post-colonial feminist scholars, who critiqued the play's cultural essentialism (Gerhard, 2000: 471).

These critiques scrutinize both the form and the content of Ensler's work, particularly her representation of women from the Global South, her conceptualization of a global sisterhood/vaginahood, and her appropriation of the suffering endured by women in these regions. The concept of 'vagina-selfhood', a term coined by Christine M. Cooper (2007: 747), underpins both *TVM* and Ensler's feminist politics, asserting a unifying bond among all women. This pursuit of vaginal 'Oneness' or 'Sameness' (Njambi, 2009: 169), based on shared anatomy, ultimately 'flattens out, if not denies, the diversity of experience within and across populations of women' (Cooper, 2007: 738). Sealing Cheng (2009: 21) and Cooper (2007: 745) further challenge Ensler's problematic appropriation of narratives surrounding genital mutilation and rape, which are exclusively associated with the 'non-Western' world. This framing reinforces a stark dichotomy between 'Western women' and 'Third World women', exacerbating the alienation and marginalization of the latter. In the play, 'Western' women are featured in acts such as 'Hair', 'The Vulva Club', and 'Reclaiming Cunt', which celebrate vaginal pleasure and depict women as empowered individuals capable of expressing feminist emotions such as rage and discomfort in response to pain. In contrast, women from the Global South are often relegated to segments like 'Not-So-Happy Vagina Fact', a distinction that underscores disparities in representation and narrative agency. This imbalance echoes Chandra T. Mohanty's critique of the colonial legacy that purportedly universalizes experiences of womanhood: 'By contrasting the representation of women in the Third World with what I referred to earlier as Western feminism's self-preservation in the same context, we see how Western feminists alone become the true "subjects" of this counter-history. Third World women, on the other hand, never rise above the debilitating generality of their "object status"' (1991: 71).

This Western-centric framing extends to specific representations of Muslim women and war-affected regions. Srimati Basu critically examines Ensler's portrayal of Afghanistan, particularly how the image of women in burqas raises questions about Western feminism's tendency to define and direct feminist movements in the region (2010: 32). She further points out that this portrayal aligns with the imperialist agenda of the US and its invasion of Afghanistan (40).

Similarly, Cooper critiques this cultural essentialism in the monologue 'My Vagina Was My Village', which is dedicated to Bosnian women. She argues that this piece romanticizes a 'pre-modern' life before rape, constructing a fantasy that exoticizes the Muslim Other (2007: 748). This pattern of representation reinforces a reductionist victim–saviour dynamic, positioning Western feminist intervention as a necessary force in 'liberating' non-Western women. Moreover, the belief in vaginahood-as-womanhood not only marginalizes post-colonial feminism but also disregards queer subjectivity. One particularly troubling example appears in the monologue 'The Vulva Club', which tells the story of a girl born without a vagina. The tale celebrates her father's determination in finding a doctor for vaginoplasty surgery. He reassures his daughter, saying, '"Don't worry, darling." This is all gonna be just fine. As a matter of fact, it's gonna be great. We're gonna get you the best homemade pussy in America. And when you meet your husband, he's gonna know we had it made specifically for him' (Ensler, 2001: 22). In this sense, Ensler's work risks perpetuating heteronormative gender ideologies by centring female anatomy and framing vaginas primarily as objects of heterosexual male desire.

Positioning *TVM* within these 'webs' of feminist critiques allows us to see the play not in isolation, nor each critique as a singular denunciation, but rather as part of a larger, interconnected ecosystem – one that links feminist theatrical events and community-based activism with a wide spectrum of feminist epistemologies. This interconnected feminist ecosystem can be understood as a 'feminist network of resistance', as Aston terms it (2016: 5). And this network of resistance is ever-expanding. As Sara Ahmed argues, 'we need to stay uncomfortable within feminism, even when we feel it provides us with a home' (2013: 175). The conflicting yet intertwining feminist ideals, epistemologies, and practices continually unsettle these 'vaginal' networks of resistance, leaving feminists 'uncomfortable' and *TVM* as a feminist text perpetually open to critique. Essentially, at the heart of these critiques lies a central issue: the question of inclusion and exclusion. This complexity is further compounded by concerns over adaptations. The underlying power dynamics underscore the importance of examining localized productions of *TVM* – produced, directed, written, and performed by local communities – which can offer more nuanced and diverse representations. As Basu persuasively argues, 'it would be more useful to interrogate ... the ways in which adding different frames based on gender, ethnicity, or sexuality' could potentially 'transform' these foundational assumptions or premises (2010: 39).

Looking at *TVM* as a global feminist phenomenon, the trajectory of its performances as part of V-Day campaigns began in cities in the US such as Chicago, Los Angeles, and New York, extending its reach to Karachi, Mumbai,

Singapore, Manila, Hong Kong, Tel Aviv, Cairo, Guatemala City, Lusaka, and many more (Basu, 2010: 38). These transnational explorations are ways in which feminists critically engage with *TVM*, examining the intersection of race, class, nationality, and other identity markers that complicate the gendered analysis in and beyond *TVM*. In China, attempts to adapt and stage *TVM* as a major form of feminist practice began in the early 2000s and remain ongoing. Numerous Chinese cultural and arts institutions, including the Shanghai Dramatic Arts Centre (SDAC *Shanghai huaju yishu zhongxin*) and the Today Art Gallery in Beijing (TAGB *Beijing jinri meishuguan*), sought to license *TVM* in China. However, they encountered significant administrative hurdles. Shanghai officials indefinitely postponed the performance scheduled at SDAC in February 2004. Just a week later, the show planned for Valentine's Day in Beijing was also cancelled. In Shanghai, the play was halted due to concerns that 'the production was not yet mature'.[4] Meanwhile, in Beijing it was banned due to alleged 'loopholes in the approval procedures', as stated by Beijing arts officials (Bezlova, 2004). Angel An, a curator at TAGB where the performance was to take place, was informed that the organizers 'hadn't obtained permission from the cultural authorities' (Bezlova, 2004), underscoring the stringent regulatory oversight in China's cultural sphere.

The V-Day campaign, too, enforces rigorous guidelines for transnational groups aiming to bring Ensler's original play and the campaign to local communities. Outlined in the 'Organize a V-Day Event' section on the campaign's website,[5] these rules are crucial for organizers. They must first register for rights to host the event, strictly adhering to guidelines on script, performance date, venue selection, and public methods. Having to navigate the dual challenges of governmental censorship and the scrupulous staging guidelines imposed by the V-Day campaign has driven the staging of *TVM* in China underground. Nonetheless, grassroots productions of *TVM* continue to thrive, demonstrating the resilience and tenacity of these movements despite oppressive regulations. Initially stringent about the script and performance dates, Ensler later endorsed adaptations of *TVM* in China that incorporated local narratives (Ke, 2019: 129). She also stepped back from a leading role in the V-Day organization, supporting activists of colour to take centre stage (Ensler, 2020).

My selection of and approach to the three Chinese productions featured in this Element uncover two crucial connections left unpacked by previous scholars: the genealogical connection between the past and the present in

---

[4] See Kahn, 2004, for a *New York Times* interview with Li Shengying, director of the Shanghai performance.
[5] See the V-Day Campaign website, www.vday.org/node/1709.html#when (accessed 20 July 2024).

Chinese feminist theatre making and the geographical connections between local and transnational feminist movements, where theatre making plays a key role. Strategically, I compare these three performances with one another and with Ensler's original, analysing the differences in their scripts, theatre organizing, funding sources, performance tactics, advertising approaches, theatre spaces, spectatorship, and levels of social engagement. A critical examination of these differences makes visible the agency and inner complexity of contemporary Chinese feminists and their theatre-making practices. Through an in-depth analysis of local feminist practices in China and their dynamic relationship with the global feminist framework, I resist the idea of 'the local' as singular or monolithic and contest its subordination to the 'global'. In doing so, I align my stance with Mohanty's argument for a 'grounded' and 'particularized' analysis – one that sees 'the local as specifying and illuminating the universal' (2002: 501, 503). I read Chinese productions not as a replacement of one set of monolithic monologues with another but as active dialogues and conversations with *TVM*, shaped by and negotiated within shifting local environments and transnational feminist dynamics. As Sue Ellen Case aptly phrases it, there should be 'Vagina Duologues' – 'not vagina denial, but vagina everywhere' (2021: 37).

1.4 Towards 'Collapsed Feminisms'

To unpack the complexities of contemporary Chinese feminism and *TVM* I draw on archival research. I have collected unpublished scripts, audio-visual archives such as recordings of performances, unreleased documentaries of the 2003 *Yin Dao Du Bai* production, and digital archives such as blog posts about *Dao Yin* and the theatre group Vagina Project on social media. With these archives, I contextualize each production politically and historically, and investigate the different feminist goals each aspired to achieve, such as facilitating anti-domestic violence legislation, agitating for online public debates with nationalists, fostering citizenship practice and civic engagement in urban spaces, or supporting private educational services to enhance the artistic portfolios of feminist participants and clients. Methodologically, I adopt a comparative textual/performance analysis to compare Ensler's HBO performance (2002) and the three productions to understand the shift of feminist focus over three decades.

Furthermore, I deploy interviews as a qualitative method to study the differences between the creative and organizational processes of each group in response to the shifting political climate. All three of these strategies will be adopted and intertwined in each section. Overall, the Element reveals a different trajectory for Chinese feminism compared to the waves of anglophone feminism dating back to the late nineteenth century. Chinese feminists' self-defined and self-organized advocacy for legal rights (loosely equivalent to first-wave feminism), broader social rights (second-wave feminism), rural and migrant women's rights (third-wave intersectional feminism), digital citizenship (fourth-wave feminism), and individual female success (neoliberal feminism) was condensed into a remarkably short span of thirty years – from the UN Women Beijing Conference 1995 onwards – roughly paralleling the timeline of Ensler's *TVM*. Crucially, from a feminism and theatre perspective, drawing on this historical analysis, the Conclusion (Section 5) introduces the concept of 'collapsed feminisms' to summarize how Chinese feminist theatres from 2003 to 2021 staged an exceptionally complicated scene in which these multiple, feminist currents overlapped and 'collapsed' together.

2 The Politics of Desire: Feminist Erotic Desires in *Yin Dao Du Bai* and (Neo-)Liberalism

Eve Ensler's *TVM* was first introduced to China in 2001 at the Hopkins-Nanjing Center at Nanjing University, and a year later at the American Club Shanghai. By 2003, campus productions had begun to proliferate, showcasing diverse Chinese adaptations. The first notable one, *Yin Dao Du Bai* (*The Vagina Monologues*), was staged at Guangdong Museum of Art (*Guangdong meishuguan*). This production, directed by Ai Xiaoming, a renowned feminist activist and Professor of Chinese Literature and Women's Studies at Sun Yat-sen University (SYSU) in Guangzhou, involved students and faculty in the Department of Chinese. The performance was co-initiated by the Anti-domestic Violence Network of China Law Society (*zhongguo faxuehui fanjiabao wangluo*) and the Sex-Gender Education Forum (*zhongda xingbiejiaoyu luntan*), established in 2003 at SYSU. Supported by Oxfam and the Anti-domestic Violence Network, this collaboration highlighted a concerted effort to raise awareness about women's issues, particularly domestic violence, in China (Ke, 2019: 128).

Since the landmark 2003 performance at SYSU, numerous Chinese productions of *TVM* have been staged by various theatre and feminist societies and organizations. Grassroots theatre groups, feminist organizations, and LGBTQ communities in Shanghai, Beijing, Wuhan, and other cities were inspired to create their own productions, extending the influence of *TVM* beyond the campus environment. Qianting Ke, Assistant Professor in Chinese Literature at SYSU, who participated in the 2003 performance as a student of Ai and later initiated the tenth-anniversary SYSU performance *For Vagina's Sake* (*jiang yindaodubai daodi*) in 2013, highlights the grassroots nature of these Chinese productions as well as their deviation from the global V-Day campaign:

> Women's organizations in China are concerned about anti-violence issues when they adapt *TVM*, [*sic*] however, they are not engaged in the V-Day worldwide Campaign. Rather than register and then wait for the newly released script, following the rules of fundraising and performing, Chinese activists create new stories based on the experiences of Chinese women. According to the rules of V-Day, the free copyright is for the V-Day period, initially from February to the 8th of March, but at present has been narrowed to February only. (2019: 128)

What made it so challenging for most Chinese groups to officially register for the global V-Day campaign? Foremost among their reasons was a genuine devotion to representing the lived experiences specific to Chinese women. The original script of *TVM*, updated annually on the V-Day website until 2020, drew on the experiences of middle-class white American women. Without appropriate localization, these stories risked failing to resonate with Chinese audiences. Compounding this difficulty was the requirement for fundraising, a crucial component of the V-Day campaign's events, which proved challenging to achieve in a Chinese context. As highlighted by Ke, 'most Chinese grassroots or women's organizations cannot legally raise funds from the public through performances' (2019: 129). Despite the compelled and calculated deviation from V-Day's rules, Eve Ensler proactively championed the Chinese feminist collectives' ineluctable departure, evidenced by her engagement with members of these groups during the Women Status Promotion Asian Conference (*funv diwei tisheng yazhou huiyi*) in 2015 in Taiwan, organized by the Garden of Hope Foundation, a Christian charity for women's rights. She fostered close ties with BCome, a Beijing-based feminist group engaged in adapting *TVM* for local audiences, whose initiatives will be unpacked in Section 3.

On 7 December 2003, a new chapter in Chinese feminism began with the premiere of the first Chinese production of *TVM* at the Guangdong Museum of Art (see Figure 1). This landmark production featured an assiduous and synergistic ensemble, brimming with local resonance through the incorporation of three evocative tales particular to Chinese women: 'Abandoned Babies', 'Dried-Up Woman', and 'Moan'. Ai further documented this transformative production in a Chinese-language film with English subtitles. It captures not only the performance but also the close-knit rehearsals and untold stories behind the scenes (Hu and Ai, 2004). In this documentary, Ai included the voices of her students/performers, along with the reactions of their mothers and grandmothers. She also featured insights from Chinese feminist scholars who framed the performance within a broader network of resistance against sociocultural

Figure 1 Screenshot of the poster from the 2003 SYSU production, taken from Ai's documentary.

barriers faced by women, particularly those regulating their sexualities. Bu Wei, Professor of Journalism at the Institute of Social Science Academy of China, believed that the show 'has a further cultural implication to it ... It challenges the cultural violence that we've got so accustomed to' (Hu and Ai, 2004). The film screening took place at Fudan University, Shanghai, as a salient contemporary feminist homage to the International Conference on Feminist Thought of the Last Hundred Years in China (*zhongguo bainian nvquan sichao guoji yantaohui*).

Ai first encountered *TVM* in 2000 while she was a visiting scholar in the United States. She was captivated by the controversy surrounding its performances across various institutions, including universities, media outlets, and religious organizations. Reflecting on her interview with the Global Feminism Project at the University of Michigan, she recalled: 'I stumbled upon discussions about the performances at different campuses and came across some production photos. It generated significant criticism, particularly from conservative commentators ... I found the entire debate deeply intriguing' (Hu and Ai, 2004). During her time in America, Ai immersed herself in feminist artworks like Judy Chicago's 'The Menstruation Bathroom' (see Bagtazo, 2018), which prompted her to contemplate women's experiences in the Chinese context. Realizing that women's joys and sorrows had long been marginalized, she saw the potential for visual expressions to render their invisibility visible. This revelation inspired her to consider integrating *TVM* into her own teaching upon returning to SYSU. In the winter of 2002, SYSU hosted a workshop on 'Curriculum Development for Women's and Gender Studies', where Ai presented an interactive multimedia session featuring *TVM* to faculty members from women's studies departments across China (Hu and Ai, 2004). Ai observed that audiences reacted with a mix of amazement and shock regarding the introduction of such a topic in the classroom. By way of this realization, the critical need for and importance of bringing a Chinese production of *TVM* to audiences in China was reinforced, beginning with universities. Recognizing the immense challenge this represented, Ai actively engaged with her students, who not only shared her vision but also committed to collaborating on adapting and staging the first ever Chinese *Vagina Monologues*.

2.1 Re-presenting and Reimagining Chinese Women on Stage

The 2003 SYSU production *Yin Dao Du Bai* comprises a prologue (*yin zi*) and sixteen acts, namely 'Hair' (*yin mao*), 'If Your Vagina Got Dressed, What Would It Wear?' (*ruguo niyao daban nide yindao*), 'My Short Skirt' (*wode duanqun*), 'Flood' (*hongshui*), 'Menarche' (*chuchao*), 'The Vagina Workshop' (*yindao gongzuofang*), 'My Village, My Vagina' (*wode cunzhuang wode yindao*), 'Memory' (*jiyi*), 'Abandoned Babies' (*qiying*), 'Girl's Q&A' (*nvhai wenda*), 'Dried-Up River' (*ganhe de heliu*), 'Loneliness and Care' (*gudu yu guanai*), 'Because He Liked to Look at It' (*yinwei ta xihuan kan*), 'Moan' (*shenyin*), 'The Dance of Birth' (*chusheng zhiwu*), and 'I Was There in the Room' (*chanfang*). This adaptation is a distinctive hybrid, as Zhongli Yu explains:

> Ai bought a copy, which is very likely to have been the 1998 edition since she was in America in 2000 ... [upon returning to China] ... she organised her students to translate the play and put it on stage ... [She then] obtained the video of the English production at Harvard University, and made her students note down and type the script separately so that each student had an e-version of it ... Compared with the 1998 and 2001 English versions, the translation seems like an adaptation based on more than one single version ... Therefore, it is likely that the translation is based on at least three sources, the 1998 version, the 2001 version, and the Harvard production (2015: 74).

Three acts were renamed: 'Menarche' now echoes 'I Was Twelve. My Mother Slapped Me' from Ensler's 2001 script, while 'Memory' aligns with 'The Little Coochi Snorcher That Could' from the same source. Further, 'Loneliness and Care' was translated from Ensler's 'Vagina-Friendly Map', featuring anecdotes from a Vietnamese American girl and an Oklahoma girl. Act 9 'Abandoned Babies' and Act 14 'Moan' depict women's lived experiences deeply embedded in the Chinese context. Act 9 is a poignant dance piece that unveils the ongoing tragedy of female infanticide in China, while Act 14 is a comedic performance featuring three actors engaging in a playful onstage competition of moaning, infused with diverse accents.

Through the documentary, Ai further connected the performance to pressing social issues, particularly the shockingly pervasive abandonment of female orphans. The film included her visit to an orphanage, where she examined archives of displaced children, interspersed with scenes of 'Abandoned Babies'. Narrating stories particular to local communities like this lends an ethnographic dimension to *TVM*'s feminist framework. Scott emphasizes that the political nature of *TVM* lies precisely in its function as feminist ethnography, with Ensler taking on 'the voices of those she studies and even tell[ing] her own story of witnessing a birth in "I Was There in the Room"'. However, when the piece is restaged as a campus production with rigid restrictions imposed on adaptation, thus preventing students from sharing their own vaginal stories, this ethnographic dimension is diminished (2003: 413). *Yin Dao Du Bai*, however, maintains an ethnographic awareness as it incorporates Chinese women's embodied experiences, such as references to sanitary products and myths surrounding menarche. Also, the three local Chinese stories were hauntingly juxtaposed with the monologue on the Bosnian war and gendered violence, directly drawn from Ensler's original. Hence, this collage resonates with women's experiences across varied socio-historical backgrounds and time periods, foregrounding both local *and* transnational women's struggles.

2.2 Feminist Affinity: Post-Coloniality, Post-Cold War Alienation, or Transnationality?

Questions arise when considering this juxtaposition. Should *Yin Dao Du Bai* be seen as a transnational feminist practice? What are the implications of this woven tapestry for transnational feminism? Does the interweaving of texts create a richer texture? Might there exist a potential risk that the necessarily intertwining yet disconnected narratives of women's oppressions, joys, and resistances – if not critically framed through a feminist lens – could obscure the post-colonial inequalities among different groups of women? In this regard, to address the limits of global feminism as a theoretical framework, Elora Halim Chowdhury deploys a braiding metaphor to posit 'the necessary connecting (but not merging)' of 'distinct strands of feminist theorizing' (2009: 53). Similarly, to conceive of *Yin Dao Du Bai* as a braided dramatic work is to understand how it is informed by the complex feminist strands circulating at the time of its production – a complexity that warrants further contextualization.

For Chinese feminists, this depoliticized tendency to acknowledge differences while obscuring hierarchies – where hierarchies are viewed as simply another form of difference – cannot be read in isolation from the broader feminist context at the turn of the 2000s. It is in a post-colonial and post-socialist climate that the play emerged, advocating for sexual liberation and aligning itself with global feminism, predominantly American feminism. This emergence is understood as part of the feminist shift in China – a 'turn away' from the statist definition and a 'turn towards' transnational feminist organizing. However, concerns arise with this feminist turn, as Shana Ye questions: '[W]hat steered Chinese feminists toward liberal feminism as its primary framework? Instead of positioning itself in solidarity with Third World women in order to disrupt imperialism in the form of feminist knowledge production, why did Chinese feminists in the 1990s prioritize connecting to the globalized world by denouncing Maoist socialism and embracing liberalism?' (2021: 796). This feminist paradigm shift in China was accompanied – certainly facilitated – by initiatives like the United Nations' 'globalizing women', evident in the '"Decade on Women" (1975–1985)' programme, 'reaching its hegemony after the fall of the Soviet Union and the Fourth World Conference on Women in Beijing (FWCW) in 1995' (Ye, 2021: 799). In her article '"Woman" as Theatre', a response to the UN Conference on Women, Beijing 1995, Gayatri Chakravorty Spivak questions the use of a theatrical metaphor to interrogate the nature and implications of such international feminist endeavours:

> The financialization of the globe must be represented as the North embracing the South. Women are being used for the representation of this unity – another name for the profound transnational disunity necessary for globalization. These conferences are global theatre. There is, of course, no politics which is not theatre. But we are interested in *this* global theatre, staged to show participation between the North and the South, the latter constituted by Northern discursive mechanisms – a Platform of Action and certain power lines between the UN, the donor consortium, governments and the elite Non-Governmental Organizations (NGOs). In fact, the North organizes a South. (1996: 2)

The 'transnationalizing [of] feminism by US women's studies' also played a crucial role (Ye, 2021: 801). Fernandes highlights the limitations of such US-dominated transnationality:

> [T]ransnationalism has now become a framing term (different from and predominantly in opposition to global feminism) for feminist knowledge of places (or people linked to places) outside of the United States. The result is that this framing device has been disciplined in troubling ways, and transnational perspectives are now disseminated and consumed in ways that reproduce the kind of U.S. national imagination ... linked to representations of non-Western women such as veiling, female genital mutilation, and other cultural issues. (2013: 15)

Concomitant with the feminist transnational turn were China's neo-liberal reforms and its burgeoning desire to join global capitalism. Transnational neo-liberalism, embodied by institutions like the WTO, 'produce[s] "desiring China"', as Lisa Rofel persuasively claims (2007: 159). She goes on to argue that these institutions 'not only cultivate an international desiring machine yielding endlessly proliferating desires for foreign goods and services but also turn China into an object which others could desire freely, without obstruction' (159).

China's hosting of the 1995 UN Women's Conference was also framed in the discourse of transnationalism. Chinese government officials saw it 'as a crucial way for China to elevate itself in the eyes of the global community because a country's level of "civilization" is measured by the status of women in the international arena' (Wang and Zhang, 2010: 56). Crucially, alongside the rise of a desiring society in the early years of China's neo-liberal restructuring, there was a growing desire among individual subjects for a novel, post-Cold War cosmopolitan citizenship (Rofel, 2007: 13). Cosmopolitanism, a substitution of 'socialist experimentation', is centred on 'universal human nature' rather than class markers (3). The discourse of cosmopolitan universalism echoed the historic address by Hillary Clinton, the US representative at the UN Women's Conference in Beijing. Clinton's rhetoric – 'women's rights are human rights' – 'gained popularity and became the dominant frame in transnational feminist activism and NGO work in China' (Ye, 2021: 804). Embodying liberal feminism's global appeal to further transnational interests, her assertion resonated precisely with the shift towards a cosmopolitan universalist ethos that characterized China's post-socialist era. The cosmopolitan desires of Chinese feminists to claim a 'recognizable universal subject of woman', as Ye poignantly writes, found the ideal moment 'to materialize' during this period of ideological convergence (804).

'Desire' thus emerges as a central concept in my reading of Rofel's and Ye's works, which shed light on the broader 'desiring' transformation that is highly relevant to *Yin Dao Du Bai* and its place in the history of Chinese feminism. Rofel (2007) views desire as 'a key cultural practice in which both the government and its citizens reconfigure their relationship to a postsocialist world' (3). Ye (2021), on the other hand, provides an affective account of Chinese feminists' 'uncritical affinity' with neo-liberal transnational feminism (784): 'The communist/socialist and Third World conceptualization of gender, which emphasizes the intersection of anti-patriarchy, anti-racism, anti-imperialism, and anti-war movements, gave way to a theorization of gender focused on "subjectivity" and "autonomy" and whose actualization relies on individuals and identity politics' (799). *Yin Dao Du Bai* can therefore be seen as a site where converging and conflicting desires – those of the state, transnational institutions, feminist subjects, and female subjects – are imagined, negotiated, embodied, and materialized.

Following Chowdhury's notion of braiding, it is the braided nature of the play, performed at the turn of the millennium, that best exemplifies the affective tendencies of Chinese feminists in the early years of China's neo-liberal restructuring. Indeed, this braided texture, as I see it, lacks the frayed edges of post-colonial tensions, where vaginal texts are stitched together without engaging in a critically feminist way. Yet to argue that this play sits exactly at the point where Chinese feminism turns towards neo-liberalism, with 'subjectivity' and 'autonomy' at its core, would be to oversimplify the matter. My concern, in framing post-socialist Chinese feminist practices solely within neo-liberal discourses, is that we might risk losing the nuances that exist within each pairing of these clear-cut binaries – self/collective; market/state; agency, freedom, and individual liberty/broader intersections of feminist resistance – which characterize the convergence of neo-liberalism with feminist strands.

This concern is palpable in 'Moan', Act 14 of the play, which addresses the question of female sexual subjectivity through the staging of mimetic moans – sonic expressions of sexual desires. Hence, I have chosen to analyse in detail how the staged soundscape of three individual female subjects' sexual expressions complicates the discourse of 'desire' used to analyse the state and the feminist collectives in post-socialist and post-Cold War China. In the performance analysis of 'Moan' that follows, I interrogate the play's dominant framing device – affective neo-liberalism – for Chinese feminist practices since the early 2000s. By 'affective neo-liberalism', I mean the monolithic scholarly critique of Chinese feminism's neo-liberal turn, particularly the feminist celebration of affection and the desires of the 'self' (of each female subject). Concepts such as 'agency', 'subjectivity', and 'individual freedom', often critically examined, are embraced and championed in Act 14, prompting questions about whether it is liberalism or *neo*-liberalism that was endorsed in the early 2000s.

In this regard, Sara Farris and Catherine Rottenberg's delineation of (neo-) liberal feminism proves particularly useful. They define 'neo-' as a process that mobilizes, yet simultaneously eviscerates, liberal discourse like 'agency' and 'subjectivity'. Mobilization and evisceration are two key terms in understanding how classic liberal feminism has been neo-liberalized: 'through its concurrent mobilisation and evisceration of liberal discourse, neoliberal feminism hollows out the potential of mainstream liberal feminism to underscore the structural contradictions within liberal democracy (with its proclamation of universal rights and equality)' (Farris and Rottenberg, 2017: 10). At the turn of the 2000s, Chinese feminism's embrace of sexual autonomy did not fully align with this logic of neo-liberalism. Instead, it aimed to counterbalance statist governance of women's issues and feminist approaches, advocating for the sexual autonomy of female subjects ('selves') as a means of – rather than a replacement for – driving social change. As I shall now demonstrate, this dynamic is exemplified in the performance of 'Moan', which challenges societal barriers to female sexual expression through the act of theatrical moaning.

2.3 The Female Selves as Desiring Subjects: Enacting Sonic Sexual Pleasures

Ai lamented a profound distinction between the American women in Ensler's original play and Chinese women's imaginings of sexual desires. The key distinction lies in the realm of sexual pleasure – the play of intimacy and the imaginings of desire, elements seemingly absent from Chinese culture. Recalling a challenging rehearsal, she described how disconnected everyone felt when discussing adorning vaginas. When she prompted the performers to imagine dressing up their vaginas, their suggestions included large underpants, sanitary napkins, the hymen, and, most absurdly, chastity belts (Hu and Ai, 2004). Though risking the generalization of sexual imaginations within these two contexts, each characterized by its own inherent heterogeneity, as well as framing Chinese women as the 'lack', thereby perpetuating the US-based feminist transnationality, Ai's concerns about the stigmatization surrounding Chinese women's sexual expressions are justified. 'Moan' gestures towards feminist eroticism, celebrating a variety of moans as forms of agentic sexual expression.

Ensler's original monologue 'The Woman Who Loved to Make Vaginas Happy' voices the sexual moans of a lawyer-turned-lesbian sex worker: 'I longed to moan. I practiced in front of my mirror, on a tape recorder, moaning in various keys, various tones, with sometimes very operatic expressions, sometimes with more reserved, almost withheld expression. But always when I played it back, it sounded fake. It wasn't rooted in anything sexual, really, only in my desire to be sexual' (Ensler, 2001: 22). Ai replaced – or, in Yu's terms, 'localise[d] or domesticate[d]' – the moaning by Ensler's lesbian sex worker with the heterosexually voiced moans of her trio of Chinese women.

The types of moan in Ensler's original – 'clit moan ... the vaginal moan ...... pre-moan ... the elegant moan ... the WASP moan ... the tortured Zen moan' (23) – were translated into region-specific moans, each carrying its own sense of humour in the Chinese context.[6] In this performance, moaning emerges as an erotic aesthetic practice, expressed through a variety of styles – be it ladylike,

---

[6] A WASP is a white Anglo-Saxon Protestant. It is a sociocultural term in the United States referring to a stereotypical group of upper- and upper-middle-class white Americans who are socially conservative and proper in public behaviour. Ensler's use of the term is a satirical way of saying that their moan is more emotionally restrained, hence it makes 'no sound'.

romantic, or even influenced by classic Henan opera's portrayal of the ancient Chinese heroine Mulan. Ai 'recreate(d) the humour of the source text for the Chinese audience' through the use of 'different pronunciations, especially Henan dialect and Cantonese'. These dialects are 'the major dialects adopted in comic skits' staged during the Spring Festival Gala, 'an annual must-see event for many Chinese people' on the eve of the lunar New Year (Yu, 2015: 152). The complete removal of the sex worker's sexuality is partly due to Ai's self-censorship, as Yu suggests, to obscure homosexuality in order to 'ensure a better reception of her production', noting that this change 'reflects her [Ai's] consideration of the social and institutional response to homosexuality' (175). As previously noted, despite homosexuality being de-pathologized in China in 1989 (Wu, 2003: 128), it has yet to gain legal and full social acceptance. In this regard, *Yin Dao Du Bai* differs from later productions organized by feminist/queer collectives (see Sections 3 and 4). Queer feminist scholar Hongwei Bao, who traces the genealogy of queer theories in China, observes:

> In the 1990s, two popular Chinese terms, among others, were used to denote same-sex intimacy: *tongxinglian* and *tongzhi*. *Tongxinglian* was primarily used in official and mainstream discourses, in which sexual minorities were depicted as a form of criminality or pathology. The disappearance of 'hooliganism' (*liumang zui* ...) from China's Criminal Law in 1997 and the partial removal of homosexuality from the Chinese Classification of Mental Disorders (Third Edition) in 2001 were important historical events that gave rise to the emergence of queer communities in urban China. (2024: 168)

Whether or not Ai was influenced by these historical events surrounding queer discourses and LGBTQ rights, the shift in context for discussion of sexual minorities appeared to be only partially realized in the early 2000s.

'Moan' begins with three women engaging in a spirited discussion about female orgasm, enacted through vocal expressions of female ecstasy. As Corbett and Kapsalis argue in 'Aural Sex: The Female Orgasm in Popular Sound', representations of female orgasm in mass culture are often 'disembodied from their visual referent', making them 'a fitting item for purely aural production' (1996: 106). Similarly, 'Moan' operates as an aural performance, foregrounding the sounds of female ecstasy to challenge societal norms and explore the relationship between sexuality and soundscapes. The performers' use of distinct dialects further enriches this exploration by revealing their regional identities and varied attitudes towards public discussions of sexual soundscapes. Performer A, speaking in standard Mandarin, initiates the dialogue with a neutral tone, embodying a moderate stance; Performer B, characterized by a rural Henan accent, represents a more conservative viewpoint;

while Performer C, speaking Cantonese, conveys a more liberal and open perspective.

Performer A (Standard Mandarin): Hey, have you ever heard that kind of noise?
Performer B (Henan dialect): What noise?
Performer C (Cantonese): What noise?

...

Performer B (Henan dialect): Oh, my goodness, how can anyone even talk about that?
Performer C (Cantonese): Why are you making such a big deal out of it?

These opening lines set the scene for a comic exchange about the taboos and diverse social attitudes towards female sexual vocalizations. Moreover, to understand the viewpoints and attitudes expressed in this sequence requires situating the production within the transformation of the 'sexual landscape' in China, brought about by the post-sexual liberation movements of the 1980s and 1990s (Yang and Kavka, 2024: 3).

Pan Suiming, a Chinese sexologist and sociology professor, frames this transformation as a shift from 'sex for reproduction' and 'marital obligation' to 'the concept and practice of "sex for pleasure"' (2007: 29). According to Suiming, this change was influenced not only by 'the introduction of market-based reforms' (31) but also by policies like the one-child family policy (1981) and the government-supported promotion of contraception and abortion (28). These shifts facilitated greater public 'openness' and awareness of sexual issues, alongside increased 'engagement in non-marital sexual activities' (22). Suiming also observed changes in the 'sexual mores and behaviours' of younger women, noting a growing 'awareness of their individual rights' and the normalization of what were once considered 'abnormal' expressions, such as 'masturbation, premarital sex ... unusual sexual positions' (30). Fan Yang and Misha Kavka (2024) contextualize Chinese *TVM* within this environment of cultural and social change. They highlight how the post-sexual revolution in China saw increased public discussions of sexuality, the 'sexualization of popular culture' (2024: 3), and the rise of sex-related NGOs (3). Performances of Chinese *TVM* became a significant part of this landscape, using 'documentaries, recitations and workshops' to help 'publicize notions of anti-sexual violence and female sexual pleasure'. However, the explicit content occasionally led to show cancellations due to concerns over 'pornographic ambiguity' (3).

The 'Moan' episode in *Yin Dao Du Bai* reverberates with the post-sexual revolution climate. The opening conversation among the three female performers transitions into a heart-wrenching story that reveals why Performer B views moaning as taboo:

> Performer B (Henan dialect): It's not that I'm making a fuss. A young bride in our village died over this. Listen, let me tell you. In our village, there's a tradition of eavesdropping on wedding nights. A group of boys played a prank by hiding a small tape recorder under the bride's bed to capture their intimate sounds. The next day, they played the recording in the village square. The bride, who was washing clothes nearby, heard it and saw the boys mocking her. She was so embarrassed that she ran home, grabbed a rope, and hanged herself.

In this act, the public exposure of a woman's sexual privacy without her consent paradoxically intersects with the intentional public performance of the most intimate and private aspects of sexual life. These contrasting scenarios reveal two polarized realities for women. The first, steeped in shame, represents a patriarchal society where concepts of chastity are manipulated as tools of control and humiliation, with men using a woman's sexuality as a weapon against her. This results in deep-seated shame and dishonour, reinforcing the harmful connection between sex and female shame, which, in extreme cases, can lead to tragic outcomes. In contrast, the second scenario presents a feminist reimagining of this exposure. This juxtaposition raises the question of the 'consumption' of such aural production and its implications for female subjectivity. As Corbett and Kapsalis (1996) ask, 'Is the listener assuming a sadistic listening position?' (109). When the visual referent is disembodied, the act of eavesdropping becomes auditory voyeurism, practised over the unspeakable shame of women. However, by re-embodying the acoustic sounds with feminist gestures and tones, the female subjects on stage reclaim their autonomy. As a result, the audience is invited to reassume their ethical position.

Audre Lorde's essay 'Uses of the Erotic: The Erotic as Power' offers a profound framework for understanding the feminist erotic politics in 'Moan'. Lorde (2017) makes a critical distinction between pornography and the erotic, defining the latter as 'true feeling' and the former as 'sensation without feeling'. She emphasizes the significance of the erotic in fostering and sustaining women's power, noting that this erotic power has been 'misnamed by men and used against women' and has been suppressed by male-dominated pornography. Lorde asserts, 'when I speak of the erotic, then, I speak of it as an assertion of the lifeforce of women; of that creative energy empowered, the knowledge and use of which we are now reclaiming in our language, our history, our dancing, our loving, our work, our lives' (2017: 207). In 'Moan', the performers employ moaning as a form of alternative feminism, foregrounding the true feeling and desire of women. It was a cathartic release from the suppression of their feelings through male pornography, such as the unauthorized recording of the woman's sex life, noted in the play. By reclaiming the erotic as a source of power and creative energy, the performance not only acknowledges but also actively exercises women's sexual autonomy.

Here, women openly perform feminist eroticism, transforming what could be a moment of vulnerability into one of pride and joy. In doing so, they challenge and subvert patriarchal norms that seek to diminish them. This performance of what is often deemed obscene becomes a powerful affirmation of sexual autonomy, envisioning a future where women's sexuality is celebrated rather than stigmatized. On stage, the three women engage in a mimetic play that features repetitive moaning, or the faking of various styles of moaning:

Performer A (Standard Mandarin): . . . I'm naturally loud. I shout when there is good food, I shout when I put on new clothes, and I definitely shout when making love with my boyfriend.
Performer B (Henan dialect): Oh my, how embarrassing!
. . .
Performer C (Cantonese): Don't mind her. Why don't we give it a try ourselves?
Performer A (Standard Mandarin): Sure, let's start with a ladylike one. 'Ah, ah, ah, darling, I'm yours, you have to take responsibility for me.'
Performer C (Cantonese): Take responsibility? In this day and age, who knows who is responsible for whom?
Performer A (Standard Mandarin): Oh, then why don't you try a romantic one?
Performer C (Cantonese): Alright, a romantic one. 'Ah, mm, ah . . . Darling, haven't you noticed my virginity has a new brand?'
Performer A (Standard Mandarin) (to Performer B): Why don't you try one?
. . .
Performer B (Henan dialect) singing Henan opera: Do you think I never make a sound? I do, for real. Who says women can't make noise? Today, I'm going to show you. Here I go.
Together: Ah, ah, ah, ah . . .

What is particularly interesting is that these vocalizations are neither embedded in sexual contexts nor accompanied by other acoustic cues, physical gestures, or linguistic expressions. Instead, these moans – though mimetic – are performed directly to the audience, standing apart from the mimetic representation of the sex scenes. Rather than serving as an 'orgasm imperative' (Frischherz, 2018: 272), or fulfilling the 'contemporary obligation to orgasm' (Barker, Gill, and Harvey, 2018: 141), these sounds avoid the framework of post-feminist sexual empowerment discourses that often construct orgasms as a right or goal (141).

These vocalizations represent pure sonic pleasure performed by three women. The moans sonically embody erotic independence, sexual subjectivity, and the autonomy of orgasmic female bodies. Moreover, they are distinctly 'vernacular' and 'regional' enactments, producing aural codes of sexuality while also generating significant humour through their sonic presence.

The 'Ah, ah, ah' vocalizations – aural codes for sexuality – create cycles of repetition that hover over the audience. Akin to Aljoša Pužar's study of soundtracks in pornography and everyday human sexuality in East Asia, these vocalizations can be seen as an example of 'sonic contagion' (2023: 874). This refers to how female sexual vocalizations function as a mimetic play: 'the game of pretending or faking, but also enacting (that is constructing, performing, and, thus, materializing) sexual pleasure through movements, gestures, and sounds' (874). These moans act as personal 'sonic scripts', expressions of individual sexuality materialized through sound. In performing their desires, the vocalizing women generate sonic resonance with powerful emotional and affective impacts within the auditorium. The audience, immersed in these resonances, is transformed into an acoustic domain of female sexual pleasure, where the frenzied audibility of the moans gives rise to collective laughter. As the performers' sonic volume grows louder and intensifies, the audience's laughter swells in response, merging into a shared experience. Ultimately, by performing 'the shock value of the obscene', the three female subjects become powerful theatrical embodiments of the 'erotic politics of feminist humor' (Willett, Willett, and Sherman, 2012: 218). In sum, their performance elicits laughter as a powerful and subversive feminist emotion, harnessing the creation of joy as a novel form of resistance.

Imbued with feminist sarcasm, 'Moan' challenges the myth of virginity and the subjugation of women's sexual autonomy to male authority. The audience is amused by the playful exaggeration of the three performers' tones and the women's explicit exploration of erotic themes, which are both unfamiliar and unexpected yet created a space for cathartic subversion. This unfamiliarity and the surprising nature of the performance forge a 'temporary community' among the audience, uniting them through what feminist scholars call 'a shared dislocation out of the customary lines of identity' (Willett, Willett, and Sherman 2012: 229). This collective dislocation, central to feminist comedy as exemplified by 'Moan', signifies a transformative moment for Chinese feminism. It reveals and makes visible women's struggles to claim their own sexual desires and pleasures, which are often used against their identities. In essence, the performance conveys that moaning, as an expression of vibrant erotic energy, belongs to women themselves. Much like Yang and Kavka's writing on female erotic podcasting, 'Moan' also creates 'an erotic sonic space that engages with feminist discourses of liberation through pleasure, erotic independence, and sexual subjectivity' (Yang and Kavka, 2024: 2). It challenges the appropriation of such expressions as sources of shame or negativity, which have been historically employed to diminish female agency.

By focusing on 'Moan' from *Yin Dao Du Bai* and foregrounding 'sexual desires' as a specific subject of analysis, I positioned the play in critical dialogue with the scholarly discourse on desire – one that frames the post-socialist state, the increasingly cosmopolitan Chinese society, and the feminist longing for an '[uncritical] affinity' with transnationalism at the onset of Chinese neo-liberalism. 'Moan' challenges this neo-liberal narrative, offering a nuanced perspective in which the urge for female subjectivity and agency, alongside the desire for socio-cultural structural change, can occur simultaneously – not as replacements for one another. Ultimately, it resists what Rottenberg critiques as neo-liberalism's appropriation of key liberal concepts, reworking them from advocating for social change to promoting self-monitoring – 'from an attempt to alter social pressures towards interiorized affective spaces that require constant self-monitoring' (2013: 424). 'Moan' stages the self not as a voluntary agent conforming to neo-liberal subject-making but as a site of resistance against a social reality that stifles individual expression. The emergence of the self as a sexual subject in 'Moan' is radical, encouraging the formation of new feminist collectives that incorporate both performers and spectators. More importantly, my analysis reveals how the internal affective spaces of the three female moaners are not simply inward reflections but rather acoustic eruptions of what has been repressed. These moans become an outward critique, defying neo-liberal notions of internalized affirmation and instead offering a powerful, collective call for change. In sum, my analysis complicates the scholarly timeline that posits the convergence of Chinese feminism and neo-liberal forces, arguing – through a performance analysis of the sonic eruptions of moans – that this convergence has yet to fully materialize.

3 *Vagina's Way*: Confronting Medical-Patriarchal-Nationalist Ideologies in and beyond Feminist Theatre

In the decade after 2003, a myriad of Chinese *TVM* productions were created by universities, theatre groups, and gender-focused NGOs. The more salient grassroots nature of Chinese feminism marked a further break from state feminism. This process was facilitated by the rise of social media-enabled digital citizenship, practised by YFAs. Inspired by transnational anarchist feminist activist groups such as Pussy Riot (Russia, 2011) and Femen (Ukraine, 2008) and resonant with the rise in global, performative acts of feminist resistance to capitalism in public spaces, Chinese feminists navigated social media for the greater visibility of their feminist bodily acts. It is this context that shaped *Yin Dao Zhi Dao* (*Vagina's Way*) and 'My Vagina Says', a feminist campaign. *Yin Dao Zhi Dao* was a student production staged as part of a Gender and Sociology module and directed by the lecturer Li Jinzhao at Beijing Foreign Studies University (BFSU). Before the performance, students launched the associated 'My Vagina Says' campaign on Renren, a social media platform designed specifically for college students. Together these events ignited a feminist-nationalist debate, fuelling nationalist resistance against feminism for its 'Western' origin.

In the wake of the ground-breaking debut of *Yin Dao Du Bai* in 2003, Chinese productions of this radical-feminist play thrived, experiencing remarkable growth and widespread acclaim. From 2003 to 2013, these performances exerted a profound influence, significantly contributing to the evolution of Chinese civil society and reshaping public discourse on gender and sexuality. They played a pivotal role in advancing sex education and demystifying women's health-related medical science. The Zhihe Society (*zhihe she*) at Fudan University in Shanghai, a drama society dedicated to feminism and gender minority issues, presented its version of *TVM* annually from 2004 to 2015. Zhihe Society's performances have significantly influenced wider communities, inspiring numerous grassroots theatre and gender advocacy groups in universities. They also inspired feminist and LGBTQ organizations across Shanghai, Beijing, Wuhan, Nanjing, and other cities, including, among many others, Guangxi Lesbian Coalition (*guangxi leisi lianheshe*), Suzhou LESGO (Les Girl, Let's Go; *suzhou LESGO xiaozu*), BCome (see later), Xiang Yang Hua Kai, and Shenzhen Shouqianshou Gongyou Huodong Zhongxin, an NGO advocating for the rights of female migrant workers.[7] Vagina Project, a feminist art and theatre initiative founded in 2016 and the focus of Section 4, continues this legacy, with its most recent performance held in October 2021 in Beijing.

Yin Dao Zhi Dao was staged at BFSU on 7 November 2013. It was produced by BCome, a feminist theatre collective based in Beijing. BCome was established by members of Beijing-based NGOs, specifically the Media Monitor for Women Network (*fvnv chuanmei jiance wangluo*)[8] and Yiyuan Commune (*yiyuan gongshe*). The Media Monitor for Women Network is an incubator

---

[7] For a comprehensive overview of Chinese productions of *The Vagina Monologues* and the communities involved, refer to prominent Chinese feminist Rong Weiyi's article (Rong, 2021).

[8] For more details of feminist NGOs, see 'Recording Civic Action in China: Chinese NGO Web Archiving Project' on the Stanford Library website, https://exhibits.stanford.edu/chinese-ngos/browse/women?page=2&sort=pub_year_isi+desc%2C+title_sort+asc (accessed 27 July 2024).

for YFAs. Under its auspices, Yiyuan Commune was founded as a civil activity centre (Wang, 2018: 64).

BCome is a homophone for 'become', symbolizing the journey to self-realization and personal empowerment. In particular, 'B' is phonetically identical to the vulgar Chinese slang for vagina, *bi*. The term *zhidao* has the same phonetic sound as *zhidao*, meaning 'knows', thereby creating a clever homophonic pun that reinterprets the title *Vagina's Way* into 'vagina knows'. This interpretation imbues the performance with a potent message: it restores agency to women's bodies, demystifies the medical science that has historically evolved at the expense of women's very flesh and pain, and amplifies voices surrounding women's health-related taboos and silence – themes that *Vagina's Way* confronts.

The vagina, as part of the female body, inherently *knows*. It *knows* and directly experiences the pain of gynaecological examinations, particularly with the use of the vaginal speculum, which forms the core aspect of women's subjective experiences. This medical instrument, with its sharp and intrusive nature, bears the historical and material imprints of medical practices that are intricately intertwined with women's suffering. The vagina that *knows* resists (pseudo-)medical discourses embedded in patriarchal ideology, including the practice of vaginoplasty for revirginization, the use of blood as a marker for virginity, and the moral-medical taboos surrounding sex. It also defies the nationalist appropriation of women's pain, which is inflicted on women's bodies by the exact same ideology. This section explores the concept of gynaecological examination as a 'pelvic theatre', examining its material traces and historicity, as well as the role of female patients within such theatre. It also disentangles one of the most fervent and direct confrontations between feminists and nationalists in China, sparked by the 'My Vagina Says' campaign on the BFSU campus and online. This campaign, a performative intervention accompanying the *Vagina's Way* performance, foregrounds the struggle of Chinese feminists against patriarchal-medical-nationalist ideologies.

The performance begins with two performers exclaiming: 'Vagina, I said it out loud (smile, relieved).' This unequivocal declaration sets the stage for a theatrical exploration of women's biological clock and the cycles surrounding their vaginas:

Performer A: Life begins here; every new-born first pokes their head out from here. We all once passed through the deep yet warm vagina, struggling, for the first time, to enter this marvellous but challenging world. (regretfully) Yet, once we leave it, we rarely speak of it again.

Performer B: We don't sense her presence, or we choose to ignore it. Until we reach puberty, each month, with the flow of blood passing through the vagina, perhaps you can faintly feel her existence.

Performer A: Or until the first sexual encounter, when a finger or penis enters the vagina, perhaps you sense her presence through pain and pleasure.

Performer B: Or perhaps, until the cold metal of a speculum during a gynaecological exam intrudes into the vagina, you feel her presence.

Performer A: And her most noticeable moments are always associated with childbirth and illness – (pauses, sarcastically) I mean, giving birth and vaginitis.

Performer B: ... People are ashamed to discuss a sick vagina, as if its illness implies some kind of moral failing.

Performer A: She is too hidden; she rarely makes a sound ... But we ourselves ... we must talk about the vagina.

Performer B: ... Not for diagnosis, not out of curiosity, but openly, clearly, with joy and serious contemplation.[9]

These vocalized complaints resonate with compelling energy, captivating the audience in the theatre on the fifth floor of the Honglou Building at BFSU, according to Li Jinzhao, the director of the performance and a professor of English.[10] This prologue resonates profoundly within the Chinese context, inviting reflection and dialogue on frequently silenced facets of women's experiences. It speaks to Chinese women who, due to limited access to sex education, reproductive knowledge, and information about women's health, have had to navigate the public healthcare system, particularly enduring gynaecological examinations (GE). This narrative serves as a collective outcry against the invisibility, trivialization, and stigmatization of women's sexuality and related illness. It critiques biased and prejudiced medical discourses and highlights the pervasive absence of compassionate care within the Chinese healthcare system. In doing so, the performance evokes deep resonance and raises awareness among the audience as it illuminates these pressing issues.

Initially, the audience consisted solely of students in Li's class and their friends, but it quickly grew beyond students from the School of English and International Studies. As a mid-term exam for the class – during which Li facilitated discussions on feminisms, gender, and sociology – the feminist play initially represented Li's innovative pedagogical approach to exploring feminist theories with students in an embodied manner. However, the performance itself, fuelled by social media and word-of-mouth among college students across Beijing, attracted

---

[9] BCome, unpublished script of *Vagina's Way*, 2. My translation.
[10] Zoom interview with Li Jinzhao, 22 May 2024. My translation.

a much larger audience than Li had anticipated. In my interview with her, she described with awe how the queue extended from the fifth floor, down to the ground floor of the building, and out to the pitch beside it.[11]

3.1 Positioning 'Vagina' in Feminist Theatre and Theories: Corporeal Feminism

Commencing the performance with an emphasis on the vagina runs the risk of eliciting from feminist scholars critiques that are analogous to those encountered by Ensler's original play, specifically charges of gender essentialism and a reductionist view of women's subjectivities rooted in biology (see Section 1). Acknowledging feminists' uneasy relationship with the body – simultaneously shying away from reductionist, anti-essentialist views yet recognizing its inseparability (in an anti-logocentric sense, where corporeality is pivotal to theorizations of subjectivity and identity) – Elizabeth Grosz proposes a framework of analysis termed 'corporeal feminism'. This approach embraces an understanding of corporeality that aligns with feminist endeavours to dismantle patriarchal structures and establish self-defined terms and representations (1987: 3), steering clear of essentialist pitfalls in theorizing or representing female sexuality and rejecting the naturalistic belief of *a prior* femininity – criticisms frequently levelled against *TVM* by feminist scholars. The challenge thus resides in addressing the body without succumbing to biological reductionism. Grosz advocates incorporating 'bodily cycles and processes', specifically those 'located in women's bodies', within the framework of 'corporeal feminism'. This approach acknowledges 'women's carnal existence' and their 'corporeal commonness' as a 'universal "raw material"', while remaining 'pliable enough to account for cultural, historical, class and racial specificities' (2). She concludes that, in feminist analysis of women's identities, we must consider the notion of the body in two conditions: as 'universal in its generality, yet "open" to any culture's particular significations and requirements' (2). Grosz's emphasis on the body's pliability as a non-fixed, non-inert subject capable of resisting and reformulating informs this section, particularly regarding the relationship between the body and women's health-related medical science.

Drawing on the notion of pliability, I introduce an additional dimension to Grosz's perspective: the body – as flesh – is materially pliable, constantly subject to probing, stretching, adjusting, moulding, and being temporally yet continually shaped and reshaped (in a literal sense) through embodied encounters with medical instruments and technologies. *Vagina's Way* delves into women's corporeal realities and their embodied encounters with the Chinese

---

[11] Zoom interview with Li Jinzhao, 22 May 2024. My translation.

Chinese Feminisms and The Vagina Monologues 31

healthcare system, confronting the built-in stigmatization of female patienthood, the carelessness of medical professionals, and debunking pervasive myths surrounding women's bodies. By foregrounding female biological sex within this specific socio-cultural framework, *Vagina's Way* emerges as a potent act of consciousness-raising and taboo-breaking in Chinese society, where enduring myths about vaginas pervade medical and socio-cultural discourses and practices.

3.2 Performative/Mimic Virginity

Act 3, 'My Angry Vagina' (*fennu de yindao*), opens with the translation of two vaginal myths from Eve Ensler's original text. Both excerpts are drawn from *The Women's Encyclopedia of Myths and Secrets* (Walker, 1996).[12] The first recounts a witch hunt triggered by the discovery of a woman's clitoris by an investigating lawyer; the second addresses the pathologizing of girls' masturbation. These myths represent biologistic prejudices and extreme forms of violence inflicted upon women. The former saw women persecuted solely based on their anatomy, while the latter endorsed brutal practices such as clitoral cauterization and the use of miniature chastity belts to 'correct' girls' 'medical problems' (Ensler, 2001: 11, 16). Building on historical vaginal 'facts' from the sixteenth and nineteenth centuries in the United States, Act 3 proceeds to explore vaginal experiences that are specific to Chinese women:

> A website dedicated to chastity? Virginity verification certificate? What on earth is this nonsense? It's as if they are treating our vaginas as commodities, something for sale, like an LV [Louis Vuitton] bag that needs an authenticity certificate to prove its value. These fools are obsessing over the hymen: using it to incite, to hype, to profit, to carve out market niches, to impose more constraints ... Seriously? It's just a piece of tissue, a membrane! Let's be clear, using it to define 'chastity' is utterly absurd; its presence or absence has no bearing on one's purity. And don't even think about flaunting it as a badge of honour – it has nothing to do with one's true worth or appeal![13]

The hymen is one of the most pervasive and unspoken myths surrounding Chinese women's sexuality, symbolizing virginity through its presumed intactness. The 'absence' of an intact hymen is often interpreted as evidence of sexual misconduct, implying women's promiscuity. The intactness of the hymen is predominantly 'proven' by bleeding during penetrative intercourse, making the post-intercourse congealed blood a physical marker of the virginity myth.

---

[12] This comprehensive reference work, authored by Barbara G. Walker – an American author, feminist, and expert in textile arts – weaves together mythology, anthropology, religion, and sexuality, offering a nuanced exploration of female sexuality through a feminist lens.
[13] BCome, unpublished script of *Vagina's Way*, 10. My translation.

Obstetrics and gynaecology (OB-GYN) medical scientists have proven that the arbitrary presence of a hymen does not reliably signify virginity, nor does the occurrence of blood. The hymen is simply 'a remnant tissue just inside the opening of the vagina that's left over from how the vagina forms during embryonic development' (Schaffir, 2020). The presence and the amount of this tissue vary significantly among women; for some there is virtually no tissue, while for others it forms a membrane partially covering the vaginal opening. Despite being tangibly real, blood functions solely to *perform* virginity within the still-viable, enduring, and perilous mythical ritual of verifying a woman's virgin status. What Act 3 discloses is that virginity does not truly exist; instead, what exists is a surgical performance aimed at affirming virginity, facilitated by medical technologies:

> Oh, that's not even the most terrifying part. Have you heard about those dubious surgeries? Just take a look at the official websites of major hospitals: [opens laptop, starts browsing] 'Vaginal tightening surgery: Medical experts explain why vaginal laxity increases male cheating'; 'A woman post-surgery said: "I finally let my husband relive the feelings of being young, and because of this surprise, he has begun to show me care and affection once more"'; 'This medical technology offers precise suturing, ensuring safety, reliability, short duration, minimal incisions, quick recovery, and a natural final look, helping women regain their youthful allure'. [closes laptop, pretty pissed off] Ugh! These are the most revolting, profit-driven commercials I've ever seen! Can you imagine it? Those women, exhausted after childbirth, their vaginas not even having time to recover, are then subjected to the risks of infection and damage, being stretched open, cut, reconstructed, and sutured again, only to be euphemistically called 'restoring "tight and happy lives"'! This is a clearly a modern form of genital mutilation.[14]

The myth of virginity transcends being merely a social construct; it involves tangible, embodied medical interventions such as 'vaginal tightening surgery', as noted in *Vagina's Way*, or the medicalization of sex, as described by Leonore Tiefer (2012: 29): 'stitching across the vaginal canal to create bleeding during the first intercourse after surgery ("revirginization")'. It is through these medical-material constructions such as hymen construction, which includes material/flesh components like flaps of skin, that something non-existent is brought into being. Virginity is therefore inherently performative, in the sense that while it technically lacks physical existence, it is nonetheless fabricated and re-fabricated as needed, often through the presence of bloodstains and the pain female patients endure during and after the surgeries. Hande Güzel, in 'Pain as Performance', suggests viewing the pain associated with undergoing

---

[14] BCome, unpublished script of *Vagina's Way*, 10–11. My translation.

revirginization as a 'gendered and temporospatial performance' (2018: 1). This material construction of virginity gives rise to a social fiction, creating a mirage of the 'virgin'.

Act 3 of the play bridges vaginal myths across different times and places, linking those from the sixteenth and nineteenth centuries in the United States to contemporary China, where these myths persist. This spatial-temporal connectedness underscores the continuous and evolving nature of vaginal mythology across cultures and eras. This Act dismantles these contemporary Chinese myths through a barrage of rhetorical questions and exclamations. This technique amplifies feminist rage and contempt, prompting the audience to critically engage with and share the sense of incredulity and disdain towards these enduring, widely held, and misguided beliefs about women's bodies.

3.3 Women's Embodied Medical Encounters: Gynaecological Examination as Performance

Act 3 then transitions to gynaecological care in public Chinese hospitals, frequently criticized for their careless practices and fraught procedures that exacerbate trauma and vulnerability in women: 'there are those gynaecological exams – what woman hasn't had unfortunate memories like these?'.[15] A quantitative study on Chinese women's gynaecological experiences found that only 57.8 per cent of female respondents in a national survey who reported gynaecological symptoms sought exams and treatments (Yang and Qiu, 2024: 1677). According to health communication scholars, these disappointing rates are closely related to women associating GE with feelings of 'vulnerability' (1677), 'dehumanization', and 'disenfranchisement' (Thompson, Basu, and Makos, 2023: 3141–3142). Pelvic examinations are linked to 'embarrassment, apprehension/or anxiety, fear, and often some level of discomfort and/or pain' (Galasiński and Ziółkowska, 2007: 477). Act 3 vividly depicts the distressing scenarios that Chinese women often experience during GEs, where they endure unbearably intrusive questions and commands from health professionals: 'What's going on? Lie down there and take off your pants'; 'You married? Have you had sex?'; 'Spread your legs wider. Also, your vagina, relax, otherwise how can I proceed with the examination?'.[16] These impersonal biomedical directives, compounded by the healthcare professionals' detached demeanour and ineptitude within the hierarchical gynaecologist–patient power dynamic, strip patients of their agency and subjectivity during their gynaecological encounters. Framing GEs as sensory and embodied performances, incorporating human

---

[15] BCome, unpublished script of *Vagina's Way*, 10. My translation.
[16] BCome, unpublished script of *Vagina's Way*, 10. My translation.

actors, props, smells, discourses, values, and ideologies, is helpful for a more profound understanding of women's medical encounters in GE rooms, as represented in *Vagina's Way*:

> But come on, facing such a cold, expressionless face and a bunch of gleaming speculums, who can relax? My vagina has been in fear days before the examination. It refuses to enter the examination room filled with the smell of disinfectant. It hated listening to the dehumanizing voice bossing it around and despised those cold instruments barging in, poking and prodding everywhere. It was nothing short of an illegal invasion![17]

The vaginal speculum shapes, in spatial, material, sensory, and acoustic ways, women's bodies. Berkley Conner states: 'Bodily space that is theoretically – or literally, as with a speculum – opened is the site of exchanges of power that constitute that space' (2021: 617). 'Gleaming', 'cold' vaginal speculums function as non-human actants, serving as props during the gynaecological performance and perceived by patients as intrusive tools. Many women experience heightened sensitivity to factors such as 'the speculum's size, temperature, and material' (Kohler et al., 2021: 7), as well as to 'a loud, painful sounding click' (Pardes, 2017; see also Nutshell, 2024), 'the shock of cold steel, the feel of sweat trickling ... [and] the tense knot in the stomach' (Houck, 2024: 10).

The widely adopted design of the speculum traces back to American physician James Marion Sims, controversially hailed as the father of modern gynaecology. Sims conducted experiments on enslaved Black women in the 1840s without anaesthesia, resulting in a medical 'advancement' in women's health that persists globally to this day (Pardes, 2017; Wang, 2024). In his *Black on Both Sides*, a book delineating the history of Black trans identity, C. Riley Snorton observes: 'his [Sims's] work signals how suffering and dominion transitively articulated the formation of gynecology' (2017: 12, 18). American gynaecology, rooted in the brutal legacy of chattel slavery and early medical practices, made its way to China through colonial missionary medical professionals, who brought with them the speculum, an instrument steeped in a complex and often troubling history (Lin, 2015: 125). Despite its brutal origins and the exploitative practices of the past, these medical procedures have persisted into modern Chinese gynaecology.

Vagina's Way critically unveils the harrowing and deeply personal, sensual, and bodily experiences shared by Chinese women as they have been and continue to be subject to the speculum. Modern speculums typically feature 'two pewter blades to separate the vaginal walls, and hinged open and closed with a screw mechanism', and are commonly made of 'stainless steel or plastic'

---

[17] BCome, unpublished script of *Vagina's Way*, 10. My translation.

(Pardes, 2017). In China, the vaginal speculum is often referred to as 'duckbill pliers' (*ya zui qian*) due to its shape – two flat, elongated blades – which resembles a duck's beak when closed, and opens similarly to how a duck's bill does. This naming connotes its disquieting impact, extensively disseminated by a social media influencer as the 'contemporary version of medieval torture devices on women' (*dangdai nvxing xingju*).[18] The term is also invoked by theatre scholar Stanton B. Garner in his examination of the intersection between theatre and medicine: 'Like torture implements, medical instruments are used by certain individuals on the bodies of others; the fact that one action is intended to harm and the other to heal does not negate the ethical issues such technologies carry with them' (2023: 31). The material presence of chilling, mechanically daunting medical devices that emit an unsettling cracking noise thus interweaves the historical meshwork of slavery, gendered violence, and medical colonialism, directly inflected on women's very flesh.

The examination room as a spatial element also plays a role in the construction of fear in women's GE experiences. The patient is seated either on a table or in a gynaecological chair, designed to hold their legs in stirrups to facilitate the examination. A sheet drapes over the patient, separating the dressed and undressed areas, reinforcing a sense of vulnerability and exposure. *Vagina's Way* offers a meticulously detailed depiction of the examination room, emphasizing how women's bodies are influenced by the sensory experiences shaped by the space. This detailed portrayal foregrounds the examination room as a theatre, specifically a pelvic theatre, incorporating essential elements of performance: the speculum as a prop, the acoustics of clicking and twitching sounds, the olfactory stimuli of the disinfectant, and the 'cold' demeanour of medical professionals, as described in '*Vagina's Way*'. A 'new theatre', as a result of the examination, was also revealed with the speculum making visible what is 'inside the vagina and cervix' (Rodríguez, 2024: 49).

For women undergoing the examination, the room becomes a stage where their bodies are subject to the medical gaze and spectatorial interests, scrutinized and manipulated under the harsh, clinical lights. The olfactory, visual, and auditory cues, combined with the physical sensations of the speculum, all contribute to a highly charged pelvic theatre. This setting turns medical procedures into surgical performances where the patient becomes both a subject of care and an object of observation and performance.

Act 3 foregrounds how gynaecological professionals assume a connection between women's sexuality and marital status, as evidenced by their default

---

[18] See social media influencer Mountain Sheep's original Weibo post 'Contemporary Female Torture Device', https://weibo.com/3626253941/OdaXTnBkX (accessed 27 July 2024).

questions 'You married? Have you had sex yet?'.[19] These inquiries represent the medical authority's implicit condemnation of women who engage in sexual behaviours outside the prescribed norms of 'proper' conduct. They attest to Terri Kapsalis' view of gynaecology as 'the quintessential examination of women', where medical examination intersects with moral judgement. Gynaecology thus transcends mere anatomical study of women's bodies; it 'actively *makes* female bodies', shaping their perception and identity (Kapsalis, 1997: 6, italics in original). In essence, GEs wield the power of gaze, touch, and medical discourses to continually shape and regulate the archetype of femininity. Specifically, rooted in broader medical pedagogy, gynaecological apparatus and associated sexual norms are employed by gynaecologists to discipline the sexualities of Chinese women. Within the medical-moral framework, these examinations delineate what is considered morally acceptable or unacceptable, thereby prescribing sexual standards and norms.

3.4 From Pelvic Theatre to Public Space: 'My Vagina Says' and 'My Short Skirt'

'If my vagina can speak, it will undoubtedly scream out: "Silence those crappy remarks! Kick out all the crude behaviour towards the vagina once and for all!"'[20] This vocal vagina in Act 3 of *Vagina's Way* is amplified in the 'My Vagina Says' campaign – a bold and defiant feminist initiative led by BFSU female students. On 7 November 2013, with the approval of the Youth League Committee (*tuanwei*) of BFSU and organized by the Women's Society (*nv shengbu*) of the university, members of the BFSU Gender Action Group (*beiwai xingbie xingdong xiaozu*) published seventeen photos of BFSU female students in the BFSU GAG page on Renren, with the students holding whiteboards bearing striking messages such as 'My vagina says: She wants to be heard, seen and recognized'; 'My vagina says: open for business'; 'My vagina says: closed for business' to promote the performance. These diverse and playful messages are in languages such as Chinese, English, and Korean, representing the different voices within the university's multicultural environment.

Initially circulated within the relatively insular online community of college students, these photos quickly found their way onto other social media platforms such as Weibo (Chinese equivalent of X/Twitter), Tianya, and Zhihu (akin to Reddit), thereby casting their influence far and wide, capturing the attention of a much broader audience. Yalan Huang collected a sample of 533 posts on these three platforms (2016: 471). Crucially, her rigorous analysis of

---

[19] BCome, unpublished script of *Vagina's Way*, 10. My translation.
[20] BCome, unpublished script of *Vagina's Way*, 11. My translation.

the negative comments sheds light on the multifaceted critiques of feminism rooted in different ideological stances prevalent among the general public in China during the early 2010s. During this period, 'hashtag feminism' surged, propelled by the advent of social media platforms. This digital form of feminist activism strategically employed hashtags to amplify feminist discourses, aiming to enhance the visibility of feminist agendas and reclaim public spaces, both online and offline (Clark-Parsons, 2019). Comments on these platforms, to a significant extent, vividly showcased public sentiment against feminism. Nationalistic ideologies, amid the online uproar, surfaced as the most trenchant antagonism against the 'My Vagina Says' campaign and the performance of *Vagina's Way*.

Huang (2016) debunked the complacent assertions of the nationalists, noting their frequent use of specific arguments: dismissing feminism as an 'imported' Western concept tied exclusively to 'Western cultures'; questioning feminism's compatibility with Chinese society by labelling it a Western imposition; and making anti-Semitic remarks by likening feminism to Marxism, both purportedly '"invented" by Jews' (475). The BFSU performance was disparaged as a 'stupid imitation' and branded 'a cultural invasion' that allegedly 'posed a threat to the virtuous Chinese traditional culture and morals' (476). One widely circulated article on Tianya portrayed the West as 'morally bankrupt' (476), deriding the perceived naivety of female college students who uncritically embrace foreign ideas. The animosity towards 'Western feminism' or feminism in general is a stark reminder of the enduring uneasy relationship between feminism and nationalism in China.

These nationalists may be right about one thing: the term *nvquan zhuyi* ('feminism') is undeniably of 'foreign' origin. Combining *nvquan* ('women's rights') and *zhuyi* ('ism'), it was introduced to China through Japan during the late nineteenth and early twentieth centuries, a period marked by Western colonization (Mizuyo, 2005: 396). Chinese intellectuals, driven by the imperative to modernize China politically and culturally, began translating Western political, philosophical, and literary works, including feminist texts from Europe, the US, and Japan (396). In 1903, Jin Tianhe, a prominent Chinese feminist pioneer, male intellectual, and revolutionary, drafted the feminist manifesto *Nv Jie Zhong* (*The Women's Bell*), often 'touted' to be China's first feminist text (Liu, Karl, and Ko, 2013: 1), advocating for a *nvquan geming* ('feminist revolution') that calls for women's rights 'to education, to suffrage, to employment and livelihood, and to human dignity', albeit within the limited framework of nationalism (7). He asserted that 'women's emancipation was part of a larger project of enlightenment and national self-strengthening, coded either "male" or "patriarchal"' (7). Dorothy Ko and Wang Zheng (2006: 465) astutely conclude that, due to 'Western' origin and the anti-imperialist context of its introduction, 'the feminist project [in China] was implicated in a problematic nationalist scheme from the start', and that Chinese feminism was at first a 'by-product of China's emulating a Western-style nation-state' in the midst of China's pursuits of modernity and decolonization (465). Revisiting the roots of Chinese feminism provides insight into the nuanced dynamics – where interests occasionally converge but often clash – between nationalisms and feminisms in China. Nationalism has opened new paths of activism for women that were previously inaccessible, yet it has also imposed limitations on their ambitions and requests within a predominantly male-dominated and patriarchal nationalist framework, as outlined by Ko and Wang (2006). As these two ideologies navigate their complex relationship, contemporary feminists experience a fierce struggle between themselves and cybernationalists, exemplified by movements like the 'My Vagina Says' campaign. When feminists' interests diverge from those of the nationalists – as seen during the campaign – their advocacy for bodily autonomy and ownership of their sexuality and sex lives not only falls beyond the nationalist agenda but also directly opposes it.

The campaign's potent feminist messages resonate with the performance of *Vagina's Way*, exemplified by Act 1 'Vagina, I Said It Out Loud' (*yindao, woshuochulaile*); Act 2 'First Night' (*chuye*) with the statement 'That's My Vagina, Not Anyone's Property';[21] Act 3 'My Angry Vagina' (*fennu de yinda*);[22] and Act 4 'My Short Skirt' (*wode duanqun*).[23] They also serve as a compelling intervention in public spaces such as college campuses, amplifying voices concerned with women's health, bodies, and experiences that have frequently been distorted or silenced. This kind of feminist intervention is a testament to women's agency and sexual autonomy, boldly addressing these issues free from the shame imposed by patriarchy, gendered nationalism, and medical hegemony.

In 2012, a year before *Yin Dao Zhi Dao* was staged, BCome brought Act 4 'My Short Skirt' from *Vagina's Way* to Line 13 of the Beijing Subway. These feminist activists strategically leveraged the performance as a catalyst for societal transformation, specifically confronting slut-shaming and victim-blaming narratives surrounding incidents of sexual harassment on public transportation. They orchestrated a provocative flash mob performance inside subway cars (see Figure 2), aimed at targeting sexual violence and abuse against women in public spaces. This performative feminist initiative captured the attention of apathetic audience/subway riders, advocating for safer commuting

---

[21] BCome, unpublished script of *Vagina's Way*, 8. My translation.
[22] BCome, unpublished script of *Vagina's Way*, 10. My translation.
[23] BCome, unpublished script of *Vagina's Way*, 11. My translation.

Figure 2 Screenshot of the documentary film *The VaChina Monologues* (2013), a ten-year retrospective on Chinese vagina monologues, directed by Fan Popo, an award-winning Chinese queer filmmaker, writer, and activist, www.youtube.com/watch?v=Z1QE3s9JoGc (accessed 2 July 2024).

conditions for women and underscoring their rights to navigate urban environments freely.

Transitioning from the most private sphere to that of the most public, feminist discourses, embodied encounters, expressions of rage, complaints-as-resistance, corporeal realities, and imaginaries resonate among fellow students and citizens via digital and physical infrastructures. These confrontations directly challenge patriarchal-medical-nationalist ideologies that persistently constrain women. The performative interventions on BFSU campus and within Chinese urban spaces, bolstered by urban infrastructures, constitute integral elements of the landscape of performative feminism in early 2010s China – elements that will be further elucidated in the next section.

4 Feminist Theatre during the Covid-19 Pandemic: *Dao Yin* and Neo-liberal Globalization

In the early 2010s, Chinese feminism reached a significant milestone epitomized by the YFA movement. The delineation of three strands of Chinese feminism – state-defined, NGO-led, and YFA – may risk over-simplification since they are intricately intertwined and interwoven in a complex manner. However, such characterization remains instrumental in grasping the distinct feature of YFA, notably its emphasis on bodily acts and playful performative interventions. These are underpinned by YFA's two fundamental feminist tenets: 'feminism is a plain fact of their daily life' (Zheng, 2016: 38) and 'The body is the scene' (Wang, 2019: 155). Cast adrift from institutional backing,

YFA stood firm in its political ethos: an ardent embrace of grassroots activism, a decisive rupture from state entanglements, and a conscious divergence from the lingering shadows of a socialist legacy, eschewing its top-down, hierarchical approach to feminism. This nascent generation of feminists evolved in a post-1995 China characterized by frequent transnational feminist exchanges and in a post-2010 era marked by the ascent of digital culture. Navigating social media hashtags as their preferred digital platforms, they transformed public spaces into physical stages for advocacy. Initiatives like the 'Nude Photos' campaign for anti-domestic violence legislation (2012), 'Bloody Brides' against domestic violence in Beijing (2012), 'Occupy Men's Toilets' for more accessible urban infrastructure for women (2012), and a range of digital and street performances in the early 2010s epitomized their performative approach to feminism.[24] Another striking example occurred in the same year, when ten college students staged a flash mob protest, 'No to "Gynaecological Examination Gate"', opposing the mandatory gynaecological exams for female civil service candidates. This performance featured students with white cloths covering their pelvic areas, marked with a red forbidden sign crossed through the word 'examination'. These forms of feminist performative activism spanned the breadth of China, from Beijing in the north to Guangzhou in the south. 'Occupy Men's Toilets', for instance, spread to multiple cities, underscoring the widespread impact of the movement.[25]

This vibrant feminist landscape faced a dramatic setback, marked by the arrest of five prominent feminist activists, infamously known as 'The Detention of the Feminist Five', on 7 March 2015, the eve of International Women's Day.[26] These activists – Wu Rongrong, Zheng Churan, Wang Man, Wei Tingting, and Li Tingting – were detained while planning a flash mob performance against sexual harassment on public transportation, amplifying the irony of their arrest on such a symbolic date. The arrest of the Feminist Five sparked a global outcry, with over 300 civil society organizations demanding their release. Rallies in cities such as London, New York, Seattle, Tokyo, Seoul, New Delhi, and Hong Kong further amplified this call. In New Delhi, local feminists staged the 'Mask Demonstration', wearing masks bearing the faces of the detained activists. After thirty-seven days in detention, the Feminist Five were released on bail, though they continued to be classified as criminal

---

[24] For example, see the online exhibition about performative feminist movements in China 'Above Ground: China's Young Feminist Activists and Forty Moments of Transformation' at University of Michigan Library, curated by Lü Pin, Media Monitor for Women Network (a Beijing-based NGO), https://apps.lib.umich.edu/online-exhibits/exhibits/show/aboveground/domestic-violence/nude-photos (accessed 15 May 2024).

[25] 'Above Ground: China's Young Feminist Activists and Forty Moments of Transformation'.

[26] 'Above Ground: China's Young Feminist Activists and Forty Moments of Transformation'.

suspects. The University of Michigan's online exhibition on Chinese performative feminism poignantly concludes that 'feminist activism is no longer politically safe. A prolonged, gruelling era that requires more wisdom and courage has now arrived'.[27] Wang Zheng, Professor of Women's and Gender Studies and History at the University of Michigan and an internationally acclaimed diasporic Chinese feminist scholar, offered a timely and impactful response after the arrest. In her article 'Detention of the Feminist Five in China', Wang regards the rise of the YFA as 'significant progress in the history of Chinese feminism', asserting that the detention represents an attempt to revert to the pre-UN conference on women era, essentially 'turning back the clock' by 'twenty years' (2015: 480). She views the timing of the arrest as a blatant disregard for global feminist movements, noting that the feminists were detained just before International Women's Day (8 March) and the twentieth anniversary of the Fourth UN Conference on Women (9 March). This was when the United Nations' fifty-ninth Commission on the Status of Women was set to evaluate 'global progress for women twenty years after the Beijing Declaration (Beijing +20)' (481). Wang concludes by emphasizing the significant impact of global feminist mobilization, including NGOs and transnational feminist communities, and the widespread online petitions demanding their release. She noted that this collective effort directly influenced the release of the 'Feminist Five', marking a historical moment: 'This is the first time that a group of detained social activists have been released all at once' (481).

It was within this turbulent feminist landscape that the Vagina Project (VP) was established. The VP is a feminist theatre initiative based in Beijing, founded in 2016 by three activists, Taozi, Yingzi, and Qingyang, in the bustling commercial district of Wudaokou (see Figure 3). This collective seeks to promote gender equality and SOGIE (sexual orientation and gender identity expression) through diverse mediums such as dramas, interviews, seminars, and reading groups. Drawing on a rich tapestry of personal experiences and narratives, the VP staged its first performance of *Yindao Shuo* (*Vagina Saying*) on 27 and 28 May 2016, at 706 Youth Space Beijing. The play was devised from over seventy interviews with Chinese women and gender minorities (Vagina Project, 2021b). Since posting its initial call for participants (23 March 2016) on WeChat (Chinese equivalent of the combination of X/Twitter, WhatsApp, and Instagram; see Vagina Project, 2016a), the VP has evolved from a grassroots theatre workshop into a versatile 'artivist' (artist/activist) feminist ensemble. The group now undertakes multiple projects, including exhibitions that showcase participants' vaginal stories or objects, the Gray Pink Movement (see

---

[27] 'Above Ground: China's Young Feminist Activists and Forty Moments of Transformation'.

⚡ 关于 Vagina Project ⚡

「阴道说计划」是一个立足中国本土的女权主义艺术项目，倡导性别平权。通过女权主义 / 性别研究理论，审视个体日复一日经历的性 / 性别相关的系统性歧视与不平等。以戏剧、访问、专题分享、阅读共学等方式实现个体启蒙及群体共同成长，呼吁社会大众了解女性及性多元群体的生存困境。

Vagina Project (VP) is a native feminist art project aiming to serve various sex/gender/sexuality communities in China. VP advocates gender equality, focusing especially on the institutionalized discriminations and structural inequalities experienced by individuals and examined by critical feminist theories and gender studies.

The mission of VP is to collect the SOGIE (Sexual Orientation and Gender Identity Expression) through different programs, including dramas, interviews, seminars, reading groups and etc. Drawing on different forms of narratives, VP encourages the gender awareness raising in one's inner self, and hopefully in the wider social community. In the meanwhile, VP calls for the public attention and respect to women, SOGIEpeople as well as other marginalized and underprivileged social groups.

Figure 3 Introduction to the Vagina Project (Yindao Shuo Jihua) on its WeChat account, https://mp.weixin.qq.com/s/buYkWeN8YLG-64Wia0UD7Q (accessed 20 July 2024).

Figure 4), and the Theatre on Campus campaign (*xiaoyuan xiju yundong*) launched online on 18 June 2016.[28] It also hosts both online and in-person play readings. Since the creation of these campaigns, the VP has collaborated with academic institutions and gender NGOs in Beijing, such as Tsinghua University and the Beijing Gay Center (*Beijing Tongzhi Zhongxin*), to introduce *Vagina Saying* to a broader audience.

The VP is organized around the *Vagina Saying* theatre project, which is restaged annually. Each year, a new organizer is elected to lead the team, and new members

---

[28] See Vagina Project, 2016b, for the launch of the Gray Pink Movement on WeChat.

Figure 4 Offline launch of the Gray Pink Movement together with the first play-reading event of the *Vagina Saying* cast, https://mp.weixin.qq.com/s/fcp9UpzrKDd2Wy0QkeGRbQ (accessed 20 July 2024).

are recruited for various projects.[29] The convener is expected to be a Beijing-based college student, either female or non-binary, with experience in advocating for gender equality and diversity through the arts, particularly theatre. According to a VP member involved in the 2020/21 project and the producer of *Dao Yin* (*Saying Vagina*, 2021), with whom I conducted an interview, previous members, primarily college students or graduates, can continue participating as long as they have time for VP activities.[30] Recruitment of new members is announced on WeChat, and these members can choose their preferred projects, occasionally covering other projects as needed. Once the team is assembled, new interviewees are brought in, and their personal stories became the primary material for devising the play, ultimately leading to the creation of a new production. Between 2017 and 2018, in-person play readings were the primary focus of VP. Thereafter, there was a hiatus; the theatre collective noted that 'due to various reasons, the VP project was on hold for a whole year'.[31]

On 26 October 2019, the VP relaunched its initiatives for 2020. By January, it had successfully reinvigorated the Gray Pink Movement and introduced eight new teams: the Women's Theatre Group (*huaju zu*), the Management Team (*yunying zu*), the Design Team (*sheji zu*), the Digital Media Team (*xinmeiti zu*), the Public Relations Team (*wailian zu*), the Event Coordination Team (*huodong zu*), the Gray Pink Team (*huifense yundong zhuanyuan*), and the Women's Voices Team (*women zhisheng*) (Vagina Project, 2019b). In February 2020, the VP completed its first-quarter recruitment and issued an invitation for

---

[29] See Vagina Project, 2016c, for the announcement of a newly elected leader.
[30] Zoom interview with the producer of *Dao Yin* (2021), 10 May 2022.
[31] See Vagina Project, 2019a, for the milestones published on its WeChat account.

interviewees to share their vagina stories. This call for submissions, which ran from February to July 2020, garnered narratives from over 100 individuals. During this time, the VP released monthly reports that detailed the progress of each project and documented the volunteering hours of all members. On 14 May, the VP unveiled the teams and projects for the second quarter of 2020, marking significant growth as the team expanded from 60 to over 100 members, and the number of groups increased to 14 (Vagina Project, 2020f). The newly formed groups included the Vagina Saying Group (*yindao shuo zu*), the Babel Group (*babieta zu*), the Copy Editing Group (*jiaodui zu*), the Research Group (*diaoyan zu*), the Public Engagement Group (*kepu zu*), the Administration Group (*huiwu zu*), and the Gender Studies Support Group (*guwen zu*). The VP has been recruiting members based on the specific needs of each group and announcing new events accordingly. These groups support community engagement, such as online exhibitions, while working on *Dao Yin*. One such exhibition, curated by the Vagina Project,[32] showcased vagina-related objects from interviewees, such as menstruation cups and blood (Vagina Project, 2020h). The other, curated by the Public Education Group, highlighted works by female artists, including renowned American artist Georgia O'Keefe (Vagina Project, 2020a), known for her vaginal symbolism, and prominent Chinese female artists such as Yu Hong and Chen Shuxia. These artists were featured in the exhibition 'The World of Female Artists' (*nv huajia de shijie*) in 1990, which celebrated female aesthetics and perspectives, distancing itself from the male-dominated art world (Vagina Project, 2020e). The return to these activities reintroduces the VP as a well-rounded feminist initiative, encompassing a wide range of events, primarily conducted online.

4.1 Collective Feminist Theatre Making during the Covid-19 Pandemic

In January 2021, as the script for *Dao Yin* was being finalized, the VP began recruiting directors who shared its feminist values and were willing to work voluntarily for the non-profit production (Vagina Project, 2021a). Each director was required to select a scene from the script and present their directorial interpretation to the entire team, which would then be voted on by the VP via WeChat to determine the best fit. This process allowed members to assess whether each candidate was both theoretically and practically prepared for this feminist theatre project. The producer recounted an instance where a male director suggested that a daughter should give a dildo as a birthday gift

---

[32] A more literal translation might be Vagina Saying Group. This Vagina Project is different from the VP feminist theatre collective.

Figure 5 Poster of *Dao Yin*, the 2021 VP performance.

to her lesbian mother and her partner. This idea was considered problematic, according to the producer, as it reinforced heteronormative assumptions and phallic-centric stereotypes, implying that lesbian relationships require phallic substitutes for fulfilment. Another director proposed emphasizing the generational gaps between a trans daughter and her conservative parents. The VP noted that this approach could risk overshadowing the core gender issues of the play, shifting the focus from exploring gender identity to examining broader themes of generational differences.[33] In July 2021, the VP released the poster (see Figure 5) and announced the 2021 performance, *Dao Yin* (*Saying Vagina*). To fund the production, the VP initiated a crowdfunding campaign on Modian, a Chinese platform for cultural and creative projects, raising over 50,000 yuan. Additional funding came from iaia Yimeng, an institute that assists arts students in applying to overseas universities. This collaboration provided not only financial support but also voluntary labour, primarily from students specializing in arts, film, and theatre, who sought through involvement with the 2021 VP performance to enhance their portfolios for university applications, particularly to prestigious institutions in the Global North. One of the students from the institute volunteered to design a stage entrance and exit in the shape of a vagina for the actors. However, this design was ultimately not used due to a change in theatre venue and Covid-19 restrictions.

---

[33] Osaki, Producer of *Dao Yin* (2021), interviewed (on Zoom) by Yingjun Wei, 10 May 2022.

Initially, the performance was scheduled to take place at Penghao Theatre (*penghao juchang*) in Nanluogu Alley (*nanluoguxiang*), Beijing, following the Nanluoguxiang Theatre Festival opening. However, during the festival, the police visited Penghao Theatre, where approximately twenty people had gathered, requesting a suspension of activities. Subsequently, VP members opted to change their plans. The announcement of the performance was thus delayed owing to the pandemic. As sporadic Covid outbreaks continued into late October, they decided to prioritize the performance for those who had already purchased tickets. However, they deliberately delayed announcing it on social media to prevent drawing a larger audience, which could have increased the risk of police intervention. These constraints necessitated the VP to postpone the production by two months, with the final performances taking place on 30 and 31 October 2021, at Beijing 5 House, an artistic space in central Beijing.[34]

On 29 March 2020, the VP launched an e-publishing programme titled 'V Focus – Pandemic Mirror: Portraits of the Marginalized during Covid-19' (*V guanzhu–yi jing: bianyuan renqun xiang*). As a theatre group advocating for the marginalized, the VP aims to amplify the voices of those impacted directly by Covid-19 and its secondary effects. A VP member remarked: 'The problems did not come out of the blue but were finally made visible by the pandemic'. The V Focus specifically highlights the struggle of women who are particularly vulnerable to the pandemic, including female domestic workers (Vagina Project, 2020c), sex workers (Vagina Project, 2020b), surrogate mothers in Ukraine (Vagina Project, 2020g), and the homeless (Vagina Project, 2020d). Despite its commitment to shedding light on those impacted by the pandemic, the VP faced substantial challenges due to Covid-19. During the summer of 2021, a surge in cases led to stringent restrictions in Beijing, forcing the closure of all theatres. This situation also led to delays in receiving parcels from outside the city. Furthermore, China's strict zero-Covid policy complicated inter-provincial travel. Members from regions unaffected by Covid-19 faced potential quarantine upon returning home from Beijing. The Covid tracking app also categorized certain areas and individuals as high-risk, which could affect members' participation in the play. The producer lamented the daunting task of staging a play offline during such turbulent times.[35] There was an ongoing concern that props ordered from factories outside Beijing might not arrive punctually. Additionally, just two days before the scheduled

---

[34] Osaki, Producer of *Dao Yin* (2021), interviewed (on Zoom) by Yingjun Wei, 10 May 2022.
[35] Zoom interview with the producer of *Dao Yin* (2021), 10 May 2022.

performance in August, some actors and lighting designers found themselves labelled 'yellow' on the tracking app, indicating close contact with Covid cases or recent travel to high-risk regions. Consequently, the VP members reluctantly decided to postpone the performance until October. Reflecting on these challenges, the producer noted that 'the blend of online and offline work modes since Day 1 enabled VP to persevere with their theatre project during the pandemic's tumultuous times'. This adaptability not only showcased VP's resilience but also underscored its unwavering commitment to advocating for marginalized communities despite the formidable obstacles posed by Covid-19.

It is in the Covid-hit, post-2015 'Feminist Five' arrest climate that I position my analysis of the VP and the 2021 performance of *Dao Yin*. Compared to previous Chinese productions related to *TVM*, the VP differs significantly in respect of its organization, funding, as well as the staged performance. In terms of organizing, the VP distinguishes itself among Chinese production teams by relying heavily on digital platforms with minimal social engagement in physical communities or public spaces. This reliance on digital formats, while not inherently inferior, often results in one-dimensional communication. The VP groups, such as the Vagina Saying Group and the Public Education Group, primarily engage with their subscribers and audience through WeChat articles. The close community interactions, like those exemplified by Ai's visit to the orphanage, the 'My Vagina Says' campaign, or the 'My Short Skirt' activism, are gone. The producer explained that the Gray Pink Movement, the VP's main public engagement activity, was discontinued due to 'tightening the environment in universities'.[36] In the aftermath of the 'Feminist Five' arrest and throughout the Covid-19 pandemic, Chinese feminist theatre has increasingly withdrawn into more private and intimate settings. Unlike its NGO or public university-funded predecessors, the VP was primarily funded by iaia Yimeng, an overseas education consultancy. As previously noted, this private company encouraged its students/clients to participate in *Dao Yin* to build strong art portfolios which would increase their chances of admission into top-rated universities. The expanding neo-liberal ethos in Chinese society has led to the neo-liberalization of the education sector, transforming higher education into an act of consumption. According to Australian Chinese studies scholar Fran Martin:

> In recent decades, higher education, neoliberal rationality, and mobilities have become mutually entangled in historically distinct ways, both in China and Australia ... and globally. In many countries, amplified capacities for the transnational movement of capital, bodies, information, and

---

[36] Zoom interview with the producer, 10 May 2022.

technologies have been instrumental in refashioning higher education according to the principles of the market, such that degrees have tended increasingly to become framed more as a commodity for private consumption than as a public good. (2021: ix)

Feminist endeavours like *Dao Yin*, inadvertently caught in the neo-liberal transformation of higher education, must grapple with the erosion of their gains – a challenge their predecessors did not encounter. When mediated through theatre, feminism is reframed as an individual asset for competition in the global educational marketplace, promising cosmopolitan subjecthood and enhanced mobility.

The show's low profile (the performance was announced on WeChat only after it was staged), reflects the group's fear of being reported to the authorities for presenting *TVM*. As the producer mentioned, 'we were also going to bring the show to Shenzhen, but somehow we got reported for staging *The Vagina Monologues*'.[37] This approach means that the performance reached a smaller audience, avoiding potential external challenges such as police intervention due to censorship or the Covid-19 pandemic.

In her interview, the producer differentiated between 'artivism' and 'activism', suggesting that the VP aligns with artivism instead of activism. She emphasized that artivism is less radical and places more emphasis on art rather than politics. She further clarified that they are not radical feminists and prefer not to talk about politics publicly: 'We do it mildly (*wenhe*), not confrontational in any way, and we are apolitical'.[38] This clear-cut division between arts and politics left me puzzled, leading me to ask 'Do you think of feminism as political, at least in a general sense? And by "mildly" do you mean that feminist politics are filtered through arts as a medium, and are thus more symbolic and representational than directly confrontational?'. The producer responded, 'Yes, feminism is political, but not all about politics. We do not confront politics directly; if we did, it would be activism, not artivism'.[39] The distinction between activism and artivism recalls the controversy over the two Chinese translations of feminism: 'feminine-ism' (*nüxingzhuyi*) and 'women's rights/power-ism' (*nüquanzhuyi*). Wang Zheng delineates the former as 'ambiguous' and the latter as radical for its 'emphasis on women's demand of both rights and power' (2017: 172). The VP's hesitance to adopt a more politically explicit term reflects its tactic to navigate an increasingly state-censored, neo-liberal, and Covid-confined public sphere.

---

[37] Zoom interview with the producer, 10 May 2022.
[38] Zoom interview with the producer, 10 May 2022.
[39] Zoom interview with the producer, 10 May 2022.

4.2 *Dao Yin*: Non-minimalist *Vagina Monologues*

Dao Yin stands in stark contrast to the minimalist staging of Eve Ensler's original production and other Chinese adaptations. Ensler's HBO documentary (2002) captured the essence of her performance with a raw simplicity: she wore a black spaghetti-strap dress, sat on a tall stool, and was illuminated by a single, searing spotlight. This minimalist approach emphasized the powerful nature of her monologues, drawing the audience's attention solely to her words and expressions. The stark lighting created a dramatic and intimate atmosphere, enhancing the emotional impact of the stories about women's experiences, pain, and resilience. This simplicity was echoed in *Yin Dao Du Bai* (2003) and *Yin Dao Zhi Dao* (2013). Although the former included dance performances, the set remained unchanged except for a giant rose screen as the backdrop, while the latter closely resembled a staged reading. *Dao Yin*, however, breaks with this tradition. The producer made it clear that although all Chinese productions embraced a localized approach to varying extents, the major difference lies not only in the degree of localization of the vagina stories – *Dao Yin* showcases a more thorough adaptation than *Yin Dao Du Bai*, which is partially localized – but also in the incorporation of elaborate scenic design, emphasizing the visual and performative aspects. Unlike traditional monologues, *Dao Yin* focuses on the interactions between the performance and the audience, transforming into a sensual and embodied arts experience.[40] It is composed of six elements: Act 1 'TA Died Ten Years Ago' (*TA shinianqian jiusile* TA); Act 2 'Flings in Her Sixties' (*60sui qingshi*); Act 3 'A Private Conversation' (*yici simi de qiatan*) ; Act 4 'At the End of the Vaginal Tunnel Stood My Girlfriend' (*yindao jintou shi wode nvyou*); and Act 5, which consists of two heavily intersecting monologues, 'My Vagina Tone Mirrors That of My Abdominal Skin' (*wode yindao shi wo dupi de yanse*) and 'Who Is Ill?' (*shui bing le?*).

In Act 1, a pregnant young woman converses with the ghost of her mother. Their exchange, focused on pregnancy, medical examinations, and abortion, illuminates the deep connection they share through their lived, bodily experiences. Act 2 centres on a woman in her sixties who seeks pleasure through casual relationships and one-night stands. It confronts prevailing societal attitudes towards ageing by emphasizing the often-ignored sexual agency and vitality of older women, directly challenging ageist and patriarchal assumptions about female desire. In Act 3, an unusual dynamic emerges between a male and a female character, accompanied by lively exchanges between their respective genitals. This act gives voice and autonomy to the genitals, particularly the vagina, as they openly discuss female desire, emotion, and sexuality. Act 4

---
[40] Zoom interview with the producer, 10 May 2022.

explores the inner life of a character named Jessica, exploring her evolving relationship with her sexuality. In Act 5, two interwoven narratives examine the complexities of vaginismus, one from the perspective of a transgender woman and the other from a cisgender woman diagnosed with genito-pelvic pain and penetration disorder. This act critically explores how anatomy and identity intersect, challenging the reductive idea that womanhood is defined by physical attributes.

From the theatre to the street and back to the intimate vaginal theatre, this journey of Chinese *Vagina Monologues* moves cyclically. This trajectory not only unpacks the shift in locations but also emphasizes the intentional use of the term 'back', signifying a transition from public or semi-public spaces like theatres to ultra-public spaces like Qianmen Street (as seen in 'Bloody Brides'), and finally to a theatre that works more as an exclusive, membership-based experience rather than an open public event. By situating the VP and *Dao Yin* within the context of feminist theatre shaped by the 2015 'Feminist Five' arrest and the Covid-19 pandemic, this analysis reveals a pressing issue that demands scholarly examination: the diminished level of social engagement in Chinese feminist theatre during this period. This decline results from the restricted access to both social and literal public spaces for post-arrest feminist theatre in China, further exacerbated by the pandemic. Section 4, therefore, traces a geographical and historical genealogy of this shifting landscape. It examines how neo-liberalism in China has emerged as the dominant ideology, gradually eroding not only the availability of public-funded physical and social space available for performance but also the conditions of spectatorship, thereby pushing Chinese feminist theatre further into privatized modes of production.

5 Conclusion: Collapsed Feminisms, Chaos, Relics, and Feminist Hope

Spanning the early 2000s to the early 2020s, the three Chinese *TVM* productions, either loosely adapted from or inspired by the semi-verbatim approach of *The Vagina Monologues* and the V-Day campaign, exemplify the remarkable explorations undertaken by contemporary Chinese feminists into the themes and issues central to the lives of Chinese women and gender minorities. These theatrical endeavours are situated within a broader context of heightened civic engagement in a post-socialist, post-Cold War Chinese society. They showcase the efforts of feminist activists to carve out more space for the autonomous practice of feminism, fostering the development of desiring feminist subjects and encouraging the empowerment of female desire. Theatre also becomes a site where feminists confront the biomedical hegemony imposed directly upon women's very flesh. Women theatre makers' practices are intricately intertwined with and responsive to the evolving dynamics of various actors, including the state, local cultural authorities, women's NGOs, international NGO funders, grassroots theatre societies, community-based theatre groups, and the private sector, all of which are analysed in this Element.

Adopting a chronological framework enabled me to unveil the non-linearity of feminist temporalities, as evidenced in the theatre productions, capturing the cyclical loop of past and present feminist discourses, subjects, and issues. What emerged were moments of continuity and discontinuity, along with instances of provisional regression, within the Chinese feminist theatre scene over the past two decades. The growing acceptance of LGBTQ+ issues and an increasing willingness to include the vaginal tales of gender minorities in feminist theatre were shown to be coexisting with the spatial and political retreat of theatrical advocacy from the public sphere to more private settings. Hence, overall, my approach affords a nuanced understanding of important aspects of contemporary Chinese feminist theatre practices, emphasizing how these both mirror and shape the broader feminist climate.

The combined analysis of all three *TVM* productions evidenced how feminist theatre making in the context of Chinese feminism's shifting, twenty-first-century landscape has embodied both the process of exploring the subject position of an autonomous citizen and the gradual erosion of that autonomy and space. Between advances and retrenches, what ultimately emerges is the way in which the rise and fall of feminist theatre as a site of political change in contemporary China reflects the 'collapsed' nature of Chinese feminism. Thus, to conclude, I propose the concept of 'collapsed feminisms' to describe and summarize the complexities of the Chinese feminist theatre scene.

5.1 Compressed Modernity and Collapsed Feminisms

'Collapsed feminisms' draws inspiration from the concept of 'compressed modernity', a term in modernity studies describing a 'civilizational condition in which economic, political, social and/or cultural changes occur in an extremely condensed manner in respect to both time and space, and in which the dynamic coexistence of mutually disparate historical and social elements leads to the construction and reconstruction of a highly complex and fluid social system' (Chang, 2010: 444). Defined by sociologist Chang Kyung-Sup, 'compressed modernity' provides a framework for understanding the drastic and accelerated transformations experienced by certain societies, particularly in East Asia, under the pressures of globalization. This conceptual framework elucidates how social structures, economic systems, and cultural norms undergo significant changes within a condensed time frame, resulting in the simultaneous coexistence of pre-modern, modern, and post-modern elements within a single society. Chang initially explored this concept with his collaborator Song Min-Young, analysing the modernized familial structures and evolving gender roles in South Korea (Chang and Song, 2010: 541). Building on this foundational work, Chinese sociologist Yingchun Ji further engaged with the concept to examine the complex interplay of tradition and modernity in shaping gender role division and gender equality in China. Ji's analysis reveals the compressed nature of Chinese modernity where 'Confucian patriarchal tradition', 'socialist imprinting, market logics', and the 'neoliberal rhetoric of individual responsibility' intersect and overlap in a mosaic, influencing the changing and perplexing dynamics of gender (Ji, 2017: 3). Feminism in China, since its inception in the early twentieth century, has been inextricably associated with the country's modernization processes, including colonial modernity, socialist reform, and the neo-liberal turn (see Section 1). I contend that Chang's concept of 'compressed modernity', particularly the notion of 'compression', which conjures both acoustic imaginations and material transformation while carrying significant metaphorical weight, is instrumental in encapsulating the post-2000 contemporary feminist theatre scene.

Yin Dao Du Bai (2003), *Yin Dao Zhi Dao* (2013), and *Dao Yin* (2021) – feminist theatres and performative activism as cultural practices and political interventions – serve as crucial entry points for understanding the compressed nature of Chinese feminism. The metaphor of 'compression' elucidates the intertwined themes, subjects, organizational tactics, spectatorship, theatrical labour, and levels of social engagement in contemporary feminist theatre over the past two decades. Encompassing temporal, spatial, and material dimensions, the compression metaphor offers a robust framework for addressing the myriad complexities – overlapping, interwoven, and oppositional – inherent in the three performances across the 2000s, 2010s, and 2020s. This intricate tapestry of feminist theatre defies neat structuring and analysis, leaving many loose ends that are challenging to fully grasp. By 'loose ends', I do not imply that feminist theatrical practices yield futile results; rather, the term serves as a descriptive approach to my research subjects. With slanted grain lines, extra stitches, crooked seams, curved stitches, twisted seams, sewn wrinkles, and raw edges, the feminist scene is imbued with tangled threads and knots, frays, and varying layers of textures, unfolding as a rather chaotic entanglement. It is in such a complex entanglement that feminists in China have carved out a distinct path different from that of anglophone feminisms, dating back to the late nineteenth century.

Within a condensed thirty-year time frame, Chinese feminist activists have rapidly integrated a diverse array of advocacy efforts. These developments are both mirrored in and propelled by several key events and feminist milestones: the first Chinese *Vagina Monologues* (2003; Section 2), the impactful landmark feminist street performances (2012), the first Chinese production that ignited nationwide feminist debates (2013; Section 3), the arrest of the 'Feminist Five' (2015), the challenges posed by the Covid-19 pandemic (2020), and the latest Chinese production (2021; Section 4). These events and milestones encompass the pursuit of legal rights (loosely equating with first-wave feminism), broader social rights (second-wave feminism), rural and migrant women's rights (third-wave intersectional feminism), digital citizenship (fourth wave), and individual female success (neo-liberal feminism). The dynamic coexistence of these mutually disparate feminist elements – the old and the new, the global and the local, confrontation and compromise, the digital and the physical, public spectatorship and private membership – is what I recognize as and term 'collapsed feminisms' in China. Similarly, as evinced by the three productions of *TVM*, Chinese feminist theatre making from 2003 to 2021 rendered a profoundly complex tableau in which multiple waves of feminism overlapped and 'collapsed' together. The term 'collapsed' encapsulates not only the compression of various feminist movements into a condensed time frame but also the chaotic coexistence of them all. In brief, 'collapsed feminisms' conceptualizes and summarizes the ways in which four waves of feminism and the rise of neoliberal feminism were tumultuously compressed into a short time span in China.

Hence, while inspired by and resonant with the idea of 'compressed modernity', my concept of 'collapsed feminisms' diverges in so far as it suggests chaos and an inherent tension between conflicting elements; 'compressed' emphasizes the time frame and the condensation of elements rather than the act of collapsing itself. It was analysis of the three *TVM* performances that led me to the notion of 'collapsed' as an epistemological framework for understanding Chinese feminism – analysis that foregrounded the chaotic overlapping of different feminist dynamics. Recollect *Yin Dao Du Bai* (2003) and the performative activism in 2012, such as 'Bloody Brides' advocating for women's legal rights, in a way loosely echoing the first wave of suffrage feminism. These performances significantly raised public awareness of domestic violence, ultimately contributing to the enactment of anti-domestic violence legislation in 2016. Broader social rights, roughly aligning with the second wave of feminism, are explored throughout the performances in this Element, encompassing advocacy for women's bodily autonomy, including sexual liberation and reproductive rights, and the challenge to sexist medical discourse (particularly Sections 3 and 4). Such resistance includes initiatives in sex education, the deconstruction of virginity myths, heightened awareness of menstruation, the promotion of patient-centred medical care for women and gender minorities, and the recognition of LGBTQ+ rights. The intersectional approach of third-wave feminism is also evident in the focus on rural and migrant women's rights, as seen in Section 2. Additionally, the right to appear and protest in urban spaces, ensuring safe access to urban infrastructure, is vividly embodied and explored in all three *TVM* productions.

In stark contrast, however, Section 4 exhibits the VP's divergence from the digital feminism of the post-2010 era, paralleling the global fourth wave of feminism, as explored in Section 3. In the latter, digital activism was seen to provoke nationwide debates and material changes in physical spaces, such as the 'My Vagina Says' campaign, which stimulated the feminist and nationalist debates, and the 'My Short Skirt' flash mob performance on the Beijing subway, advocating for safer urban commuting for women. Performative feminist interventions such as 'Nude Photos against Domestic Violence' and 'Bloody Brides' also collectively sparked profound anti-domestic violence discussions both in digital forums and within urban public spaces. However, in Section 4, analysis of *Dao Yin* showed how digital technologies replaced public engagement in physical spaces, a shift partly necessitated by the Covid-19 pandemic as well as the aftermath of the 'Feminist Five' arrest. Transitioning from street theatre to a more intimate and de-politicized practice signifies a strategic compromise on the part of Chinese feminist theatre. Spectatorship can no longer take the form of a direct, unmediated interaction, as exemplified by 'Bloody Brides' witnessed on Qianmen Street. Rather, it is restricted to a private, membership-styled, intimate mode of engagement, as shown by the production of *Dao Yin*. This shift is marked by performances announced only post facto, a strategic manoeuvre by the VP that underscores the restricted public, social, and political access in contemporary feminist activism in China.

In terms of funding, the performances analysed in this Element reflect a diverse array of financial support sources, illustrating the evolving landscape of feminist theatre in China. Notably, while earlier productions benefited from public funding, the performances in Section 4 mark a significant transition towards crowdfunding and private capital. This demonstrates a move towards neo-liberal feminism, where the political objectives of feminist theatre are increasingly transformed to emphasize individual success and neo-liberal educational globalization – a shift that Yanhua Huang and Zixi Liu critique as promoting 'individualism without feminism' (Huang and Liu, 2022: 1027).

In sum, the progression and regression, the advances and setbacks, the persistence and interruptions, the continuity and discontinuity in the pursuit of radical feminism, and the chaotic coexistence of various waves of feminism over the past two decades have collectively shaped a fragmented and non-linear progressive trajectory for contemporary feminist theatre in China.

5.2 Beyond Collapsed Feminisms: Seeking Feminist Hope in the Relics

'This recurrent rhetoric of the past in the present has implications for feminist futures', as Sara Ahmed (2003: 236) aptly observes. '[T]he question of "feminist futures" cannot be asked without reference to the pasts and presents of different feminisms ... [F]eminism itself exists as a critique of past conditions specifically to ensure that the future does not repeat those conditions', Ahmed continues (236). While this framework of past–present–future linearity is insightful, the Chinese context of feminism and feminist theatre does not neatly follow this repetition of the past, leaving the future uncertain. What shape will Chinese feminism and feminist theatre take in the post-2021 era? Can we still maintain hope for the future of feminist movements? To borrow Ahmed's provocative question: does feminism have a future?

Feminist hope resides in the very forms of performative feminist resistance that endure and persist. As Chinese feminist activists retreated from the streets, subways, and theatres, they fully leveraged digital technologies to continue their advocacy, amplify civic engagement, and, at times, confront the state. Utilizing hashtags on Weibo, they increased visibility for issues where women's rights and bodily autonomy were threatened. For instance, their battle with gendered nationalism persisted, notably through their acts against the notoriously performative 'head-shaving' of female healthcare professionals[41] and the creation of gendered nationalist propagandist digital avatars during the Covid-19 pandemic (Wei, 2022: 359, 371). In particular, they effectively used social media platforms for their anti-domestic violence advocacy. Their digital initiatives provoked material changes in physical spaces, reconfiguring Covid-constrained neighbourhoods into sites of feminist resistance against domestic violence and gendered restrictions (Wei, 2023: 111–112). The recurring challenges of domestic violence, despite the effective advocacy by feminists for the

---

[41] During the early stages of the Covid-19 outbreak in China, a group of female nurses in Gansu Province were filmed having their heads shaved. It was intended to symbolize their commitment to the frontline, although the fact that many were crying suggests that they were not entirely willing. This sparked backlash from digital feminist activists, who accused the local government of infringing female healthcare professionals' bodily autonomy for nationalist purposes. Female health workers also faced inadequate care, such as lacking sanitary products. Two gendered nationalist avatars were created, one of which, named *Jiangshanjiao*, represents unity in the fight against the crisis. Digital feminists later reappropriated this avatar as a symbol of resistance, with slogans like '*Jiangshanjiao*, do you get your period?', demanding justice for female healthcare workers.

anti-domestic violence law enacted in 2015 and implemented in 2016, and the ongoing struggles against gendered nationalism, which Chinese feminists have long contested, illustrate the inherent necessity for activists to simultaneously navigate multiple temporalities: past, present, and future. This dynamic is intrinsic to the nature of Chinese feminist work. By explicitly addressing these intertwined and collapsed temporalities, feminists unlock the potential to shape and continually reshape the future.

In seeking hope amid the temporary yet productive chaos of Chinese feminism, the role of feminist scholars becomes crucial. As Elaine Aston compellingly argues:

> If feminist energies are gaining momentum; if the balance has tipped against feminism's neoliberal double, as campaigns such as One Billion or Everyday Sexism appear to suggest; and if there is a will to stand up and to feel part of something and to 'stop shit things happening', then for the feminist critic to devote her labour to tracing the cracks that theatre makes in the neoliberal system, however tiny or fragile, to understand how they form, resonate and link up, is also to play a supporting role in this 'network of resistance'. (2016: 17)

This Element is indeed a part of this feminist network of resistance.

References

Ahmed, S. (2003) Feminist Futures, in Eagleton, M. (ed.) *A Concise Companion to Feminist Theory*. Malden, MA: Blackwell Publishing, pp. 236–254.

Ahmed, S. (2013) *The Cultural Politics of Emotion*. Edinburgh: Edinburgh University Press.

Ai, Xiaoming (2020) Interview with the Global Feminisms Project (*quanqiu nvquanzhuyi koushushi*), https://sites.lsa.umich.edu/globalfeminisms/wp-content/uploads/sites/787/2020/05/aixiaoming_m.pdf (accessed 21 July 2024).

Aston, E. (2003) *Feminist Views on the English Stage: Women Playwrights, 1990–2000*. Cambridge: Cambridge University Press.

Aston, E. (2016) Agitating for Change: Theatre and a Feminist 'Network of Resistance', *Theatre Research International*, 41(1), pp. 5–20.

Bagtazo, C. (2018) Female Study: Judy Chicago's Menstruation Bathroom, blog, *Bagtazo*, www.bagtazocollection.com/blog/menstruationbathroom (accessed 21 July 2024).

Bao, H. W. (2024) When Queer Theory Speaks Chinese: Translating Queer Theory in China, in Zhao, J. J. and Bao, H. (eds.) *Routledge Handbook of Chinese Gender and Sexuality*. Abingdon: Routledge, pp. 165–179.

Barker, M. J., Gill, R. and Harvey, L. (2018) Mediated Intimacy: Sex Advice in Media Culture, *Sexualities*, 21(8), pp. 1337–1345.

Barlow, T. (2004) *The Question of Women in Chinese Feminism*. Durham, NC: Duke University Press.

Basu, S. (2010) V is for Veil, V is for Ventriloquism: Global Feminisms in *The Vagina Monologues*, *Frontiers: A Journal of Women Studies*, 31(1), pp. 31–62.

Bell, S. E. and Reverby, S. M. (2005) Vaginal Politics: Tensions and Possibilities in *The Vagina Monologues*, *Women's Studies International Forum*, 28(5), pp. 430–444.

Bezlova, A. (2004) Valentine's Yes, but not 'Vagina Monologues', IPS (Inter Press Service) News Agency, 17 February, www.ipsnews.net/2004/02/arts-weekly-china-valentines-yes-but-not-vagina-monologues/ (accessed 20 July 2024).

Case, S.-E. (2021) Butch Woman: A Meditation, in Rosenberg, T., D'Urso, S. and Winget, A. R. (eds.) *The Palgrave Handbook of Queer and Trans Feminisms in Contemporary Performance*. Basingstoke: Palgrave Macmillan, pp. 27–40.

Chang, K. S. (2010) The Second Modern Condition? Compressed Modernity as Internalized Reflexive Cosmopolitization, *British Journal of Sociology*, 61(3), pp. 444–464.

Chang, K. S. and Song, M. Y. (2010) The Stranded Individualizer under Compressed Modernity: South Korean Women in Individualization without Individualism, *British Journal of Sociology*, 61(3), pp. 539–564.

Cheng, S. (2009) Questioning Global Vaginahood: Reflections from Adapting *The Vagina Monologues* in Hong Kong, *Feminist Review*, 92(1), pp. 19–35.

Chowdhury, E. H. (2009) Locating Global Feminisms Elsewhere: Braiding US Women of Color and Transnational Feminisms, *Cultural Dynamics*, 21(1), pp. 51–78.

Clark-Parsons, R. (2019) 'I See You, I Believe You, I Stand With You': #MeToo and the Performance of Networked Feminist Visibility, *Feminist Media Studies*, 21(3), pp. 1–19.

Conner, B. (2021) Mapping Redesign: Gynecological Neoliberalism and the Spatiality of Project Yona's Speculum, *Women's Studies in Communication*, 44(4), pp. 611–631.

Cooper, C. M. (2007) Worrying About Vaginas: Feminism and Eve Ensler's *The Vagina Monologues*, *Signs: Journal of Women in Culture and Society*, 32(3), pp. 727–758.

Corbett, J. and Kapsalis, T. (1996) Aural Sex: The Female Orgasm in Popular Sound, *TDR (The Drama Review)*, 40(3), pp. 102–111.

Dolan, J. (1988) *The Feminist Spectator as Critic*. Ann Arbor: University of Michigan Press.

Ensler, E. (2001) *The Vagina Monologues: The V-Day Edition*. New York: Villard Books.

Ensler, E. (2002) *The Vagina Monologues*, HBO documentary, www.hbo.com/movies/the-vagina-monologues (accessed 20 July 2024). Also available on Google Play, at https://play.google.com/store/movies/details/The_Vagina_Monologues?id=HUQEJswUiZU&hl=en&gl=US&pli=1.

Ensler, E. (2020) Dear Activists, a Letter from V, *V-Day*, 1 October, www.vday.org/2020/10/01/dear-activists-a-letter-from-v/ (accessed 20 July 2024).

Farris, S. and Rottenberg, C. (2017) Introduction: Righting Feminism, *New Formations: A Journal of Culture/Theory/Politics*, 91(1), pp. 5–15.

Fernandes, L. (2013) *Transnational Feminism in the United States: Knowledge, Ethics, and Power*. New York: New York University Press.

Fincher, L. H. (2014) *Leftover Women: The Resurgence of Gender Inequality in China*. London: Zed Books.

Frischherz, M. (2018) Listening to Orgasm: Hearing Pleasure Sounds in the Normative Noise, *Argumentation and Advocacy*, 54(4), pp. 270–286.

Galasiński, D. and Ziółkowska, J. (2007) Gender and the Gynecological Examination: Women's Identities in Doctors' Narratives, *Qualitative Health Research*, 17(4), pp. 477–488.

Gallo-Cruz, S. and Tulinski, H. (2020) Restaging Women's Sexual Politics: Receptivity and Resistance to *The Vagina Monologues* Movement, *Feminist Formations*, 32(2), pp. 207–234.

Garner Jr, S. B. (2023) *Theatre and Medicine*. London: Bloomsbury Publishing.

Gerhard, J. (2000) Revisiting 'the Myth of the Vaginal Orgasm': The Female Orgasm in American Sexual Thought and Second Wave Feminism, *Feminist Studies*, 26(2), pp. 449–476.

Grosz, E. (1987) Notes towards a Corporeal Feminism, *Australian Feminist Studies*, 2(5), pp. 1–16.

Güzel, H. (2018) Pain as Performance: Re-virginisation in Turkey, *Medical Humanities*, 44(2), pp. 89–95.

Houck, J. A. (2024) *Looking through the Speculum: Examining the Women's Health Movement*. Chicago, IL: University of Chicago Press.

Hu, J. and Ai, X. (2004) *The Vagina Monologue: Stories Behind the Scenes*.

Hu, Y. (2020) Feminism in Twentieth-Century China: Modernity, Gender, and State, in Liu, J. and Yamashita, J. (eds.) *Routledge Handbook of East Asian Gender Studies*. Abingdon: Routledge, pp. 106–119.

Hu, Y. (2023) Nora in China, in Zhang, Y. (ed.) *A World History of Chinese Literature*. Abingdon: Routledge, pp. 288–296.

Huang, Y. (2016) War on Women: Interlocking Conflicts within *The Vagina Monologues* in China, *Asian Journal of Communication*, 26(5), pp. 466–484.

Huang, Y. and Liu, Z. (2022) Pursuing Individualism without Feminism: Leisure Life and Gender Politics of Young Female Bar-Goers in Urban China, *British Journal of Sociology*, 73(5), pp. 1025–1037.

Jacobs, K. (2016) Disorderly Conduct: Feminist Nudity in Chinese Protest Movements, *Sexualities*, 19(7), 819–835.

Ji, Y. (2017) A Mosaic Temporality: New Dynamics of the Gender and Marriage System in Contemporary Urban China, *Temporalités: Revue de sciences sociales et humaines*, 26, pp. 1–19.

Kahn, J. (2004) Beijing Journal; Offended by the V-Word, China Mutes 'Monologues', *New York Times*, 13 February, www.nytimes.com/2004/02/13/world/beijing-journal-offended-by-the-v-word-china-mutes-monologues.html (accessed 20 July 2024).

Kapsalis, T. (1997) *Public Privates: Performing Gynecology from Both Ends of the Speculum*. Durham, NC: Duke University Press.

Ke, Q. T. (2019) How Can a Radical Sexual Play Work in a 'Conservative' Community? The Adaptation and Recreation of *The Vagina Monologues* in China, in Wu, G., Feng, Y. and Lansdowne, H. (eds.) *Gender Dynamics, Feminist Activism and Social Transformation in China*. Abingdon: Routledge, pp. 123–143.

Ko, D. and Wang, Z. (2006) Introduction: Translating Feminisms in China, *Gender and History*, 18(3), pp. 463–471.

Kohler, R. E., Roncarati, J. S., Aguiar, A., Chatterjee, P., Gaeta, J., Viswanath, K. and Henry, C. (2021) Trauma and Cervical Cancer Screening among Women Experiencing Homelessness: A Call for Trauma-Informed Care, *Women's Health*, 17, pp. 1–10.

Li, J. and Li, X. (2017) Media as a Core Political Resource: The Young Feminist Movements in China, *Chinese Journal of Communication*, 10(1), pp. 54–71.

Lin, S. (2015) The Female Hand: The Making of Western Medicine for Women in China, 1880s–1920s. PhD thesis, Columbia University.

Liu, L. H., Karl, R. E. and Ko, D., eds. (2013) *The Birth of Chinese Feminism: Essential Texts in Transnational Theory*. New York: Columbia University Press.

Liu, W., Huang, A. and Ma, J. (2015) Young Activists, New Movements: Contemporary Chinese Queer Feminism and Transnational Genealogies, *Feminism and Psychology*, 25(1), pp. 11–17.

Lorde, A. (2017) Uses of the Erotic: The Erotic as Power, in Scott, B. K., Cayleff, S. E., Donadey, A. and Lara, I. (eds.) *Women in Culture: An Intersectional Anthology for Gender and Women's Studies*. Chichester: Wiley Blackwell, pp. 205–209.

Martin, F. (2021) *Dreams of Flight: The Lives of Chinese Women Students in the West*. Durham, NC: Duke University Press.

McCaughey, M. (2013) Victim Vaginas: The V-Day Campaign and the Vagina as Symbol of Female Vulnerability, *Women's Studies*, 42(8), pp. 923–935.

Milwertz, C. (2003) Activism against Domestic Violence in the People's Republic of China, *Violence against Women*, 9(6), pp. 630–654.

Milwertz, C. and Bu, W. (2007) Non-governmental Organizing for Gender Equality in China, *International Journal of Human Rights*, 11(1–2), pp. 131–149.

Mizuyo, S. (2005) 近代中国的女权观念 [The Development of the Concept of Women's Rights in Modern China], in Wang, Z. and Gao, Y. (eds.) 女权主义在中国的翻译历程 [*Translating Feminisms in China*]. Shanghai: Fudan University Press, pp. 37–57.

Mohanty, C. T. (1991) Under Western Eyes: Feminist Scholarship and Colonial Discourses, in Mohanty, C., Russo, A. and Torres, L. (eds.) *Third World Women and the Politics of Feminism*. Bloomington: Indiana University Press, pp. 51–80.

Mohanty, C. T. (2002) 'Under Western Eyes' Revisited: Feminist Solidarity through Anticapitalist Struggles, *Signs: Journal of Women in Culture and Society*, 28(2), pp. 499–535.

Njambi, W. N. (2009) 'One Vagina to Go': Eve Ensler's Universal Vagina and Its Implications for African Women, *Australian Feminist Studies*, 24(60), pp. 167–180.

Nutshell (2024) *rang wushu nvxing haipa de 'yazuiqian', daodi youmeiyou daiti gongju?* [Are There Any Alternative Tools to the 'Duckbill Pliers' That Scare Countless Women?], *Peng Pai (The Paper)*, 13 May, https://m.thepaper.cn/newsDetail_forward_27352265 (accessed 27 July 2024).

Pardes, A. (2017) The Speculum Finally Gets a Modern Redesign, *Wired*, 5 October, www.wired.com/story/the-speculum-finally-gets-a-modern-redesign/ (accessed 27 July 2024).

Pužar, A. (2023) Soundtracks of Human Mimetic Sexual Play: The Case of East Asian Regional Sexual Vernacular, *Sexualities*, 26(8), pp. 873–892.

Reiser, A. (2006) Our Vaginas, Not Ourselves: A Critical Analysis of *The Vagina Monologues*, *MP: An Online Feminist Journal*, 1(4). https://academinist.org/wp-content/uploads/2010/06/Reiser.pdf.

Rodríguez, V. (2024) The Uber-Performing Uterus of Henrietta Lacks and Eve Ensler: Ecologies of the Womb in Mojisola Adebayo's *Family Tree* and Eve Ensler's *In the Body of the World*, in Bouchard, G. and Mermikides, A. (eds.) *The Routledge Companion to Performance and Medicine*. New York: Routledge, pp. 45–56.

Rofel, L. (2007) *Desiring China: Experiments in Neoliberalism, Sexuality, and Public Culture*. Durham, NC: Duke University Press.

Rong, W. (2021) *The Vagina Monologues*' Journey in Mainland China, *Feminism*, 21 April, https://chinesefeminism.org/2021/04/21/%E3%80%8A%E9%98%B4%E9%81%93%E7%8B%AC%E7%99%BD%E3%80%8B%E5%9C%A8%E4%B8%AD%E5%9B%BD%E5%A4%A7%E9%99%86%E7%9A%84%E6%97%85%E8%A1%8C-%E4%B8%8A%E7%AF%87/ (accessed 27 July 2024).

Rosenberg, T. (2016) *Don't Be Quiet, Start a Riot! Essays on Feminism and Performance*. Stockholm: Stockholm University Press.

Rottenberg, C. (2013) The Rise of Neoliberal Feminism, *Cultural Studies*, 28(3), pp. 418–437.

Schaffir, J. (2020) The Hymen's Tale: Myths and Facts About the Hymen, *Ohio State University, Health & Discovery*, 20 February, https://health.osu.edu/health/ob-gyn/myths-and-facts-about-hymen (accessed 25 July 2024).

Scott, S. (2003) Been There, Done That: Paving the way for *The Vagina Monologues*, *Modern Drama*, 46(3), pp. 404–423.

Snorton, C. R. (2017) *Black on Both Sides: A Racial History of Trans Identity*. Minneapolis: University of Minnesota Press.

So, A. Y. and Chu, Y. W. (2012) The Transition from Neoliberalism to State Neoliberalism in China at the Turn of the Twenty-First Century, in Chang, K. S., Ben F. and Linda W. (eds.) *Developmental Politics in Transition: The Neoliberal Era and Beyond*. Basingstoke: Palgrave Macmillan, pp. 166–187.

Spivak, G. C. (1996) Woman as Theatre: United Nations Conference on Women, Beijing 1995, *Radical Philosophy*, 75, pp. 2–4.

Suiming, P. (2007) Transformations in the Primary Life Cycle: The Origins and Nature of China's Sexual Revolution, in Jeffreys, E. (ed.) *Sex and Sexuality in China*. Abingdon: Routledge, pp. 29–50.

Thompson, C. M., Babu, S. and Makos, S. (2023) Women's Experiences of Health-Related Communicative Disenfranchisement, *Health Communication*, 38(14), pp. 3135–3146.

Tiefer, L. (2012) The 'New View' Campaign: A Feminist Critique of Sex Therapy and an Alternative Vision, in Kleinplatz, P. J. (ed.) *New Directions in Sex Therapy*. New York: Routledge, pp. 21–35.

Vagina Project (2016a) Call for Vagina Storytellers (*Vagina Project yindao gushi jiangshuren zhengji*), 23 March, https://mp.weixin.qq.com/s/Ey3qrhGmbQ5lus5NocSkWw (accessed 20 July 2024).

Vagina Project (2016b) Dusty Pink Campaign!, 18 June, https://mp.weixin.qq.com/s/fcp9UpzrKDd2Wy0QkeGRbQ (accessed 17 July 2024).

Vagina Project (2016c) 'Tao Shuo Project' 2017 New Leader Recruitment for Core Team Members, 1 August, https://mp.weixin.qq.com/s/WJ6R8UUprukiKtV13Z-CJg (accessed 20 July 2024).

Vagina Project (2019a) VP Chronicle & VPer's Review, 20 October, https://mp.weixin.qq.com/s/TsilHRePRBHuVlfPUP2How (accessed 20 July 2024).

Vagina Project (2019b) VP Is About to Set Sail Again, and We Welcome You to Join Us!, 26 October, https://mp.weixin.qq.com/s/DEg-jUnYMo2kPdv56Wws7w (accessed 20 July 2024).

Vagina Project (2020a) V Popular Science | The Beginning and Establishment of Western Feminist Art (Part 1) (*V kepu: xifang nvxing zhuyi yishu de mengya yu queli (yi)*), 17 March, https://mp.weixin.qq.com/s/1acZwOuS0lmvuse3jB1qcg (accessed 20 July 2024).

Vagina Project (2020b) V Focus | Pandemic Mirror: Portraits of the Marginalized – Sex Workers (*V guangzhou–yijing: bianyuanrenqunxiang xingongzuozhe pian*), 26 March, https://mp.weixin.qq.com/s/Z4lzlZK-Wzv6LiBX6l2Ptw (accessed 20 July 2024).

Vagina Project (2020c) V Focus | Pandemic Mirror: Portraits of the Marginalized – Domestic Workers (*V guangzhou–yijing: bianyuanrenqun xiang jiatingyonggong pian*), 29 March, https://mp.weixin.qq.com/s/GRcXCg6IYowbtzmiiV_qHw (accessed 20 July 2024).

Vagina Project (2020d) V Focus | Pandemic Mirror: Portraits of the Marginalized – Homeless (*V guangzhou–yijing: bianyuanrenqunxiang liulangzhe pian*), 19 April, https://mp.weixin.qq.com/s/vbLqQzMU0NXQhh66eJonfg (accessed 20 July 2024).

Vagina Project (2020e) Chinese Women's Art: The World of Female Painters (*zhongguo nvxing yishu: nv huajia de shijie*), *VaginaProject*, 5 May, https://mp.weixin.qq.com/s/465evoldSdUkXcQFT4c3RQ (accessed 20 July 2024).

Vagina Project (2020f) About Us | Introducing the VP2020 Season 2 Team Update!, 14 May, https://mp.weixin.qq.com/s/Gn26inqB_vOJvh1YiIYbhA (accessed 20 July 2024).

Vagina Project (2020g) V Focus | Pandemic Mirror: Portraits of the Marginalized – Ukraine Surrogacy Industry (*V guangzhou–yijing: bianyuanrenqunxiang wukelan daiyun hangye pian*), 6 June, https://mp.weixin.qq.com/s/CemPuvGcd0ElRSHLshvyAQ (accessed 20 July 2024).

Vagina Project (2020h) Vaginal Daily Life | Sex Flows Through the Body Like Blood (*yindao richang: ruxueyeban zai shentinei liudong de xingbie*), 16 December, https://mp.weixin.qq.com/s/qg-2bCFOxBBVt_cOuI996g (accessed 20 July 2024).

Vagina Project (2021a) Recruiting Drama Directors | 'Vagina Theory' ver.2021, 30 January, https://mp.weixin.qq.com/s/tYzquv4VVlG3p_UPDA1-2Q (accessed 20 July 2024).

Vagina Project (2021b) VP Theatre Preparation Diary (*VP xiju choubei riji*), 4 June, https://mp.weixin.qq.com/s/gAIYJ3OCA53A4CgU5OLszA (accessed 20 July 2024).

Walker, B. G. (1996) *The Women's Encyclopedia of Myths and Secrets*. New York: Castle Books.

Wang, D. (2019) Radical Feminist Disruption in China: A Case of Topless for the 2012 Anti-domestic Law Petition, in Wu, G., Feng, Y. and Lansdowne, H. (eds.) *Gender Dynamics, Feminist Activism, and Social Transformation in China*. Abingdon: Routledge, pp. 144–165.

Wang, Q. (2018) Young Feminist Activists in Present-Day China: A New Feminist Generation?, *China Perspectives*, 3, pp. 59–68.

Wang, Q. (2024) *fuke jiancha de yazuiqian weishenme xiang 'xingju' yiyang?* [Why Do Duckbill Forceps Used for Gynaecological Examinations Look Like 'Torture Instruments'?], *Shanghai Xinmin Weekly*, 22 May, https://new.qq.com/rain/a/20240522A09QRJ00 (accessed 27 July 2024).

Wang, Z. (2005) 'State Feminism'? Gender and Socialist State Formation in Maoist China, *Feminist Studies*, 31(3), pp. 519–551.

Wang, Z. (2015) Detention of the Feminist Five in China, *Feminist Studies*, 41(2), pp. 476–482.

Wang, Z. (2017) Feminist Struggles in a Changing China, in Basu, A. (ed.) *Women's Movements in the Global Era*. Abingdon: Routledge, pp. 155–181.

Wang, Z. and Zhang, Y. (2010) Global Concepts, Local Practices: Chinese Feminism since the Fourth UN Conference on Women, *Feminist Studies*, 36(1), pp. 40–70.

Wei, Y. (2022) Performing Gendered Disaster Nationalism and Its Feminist Resistance in China during the Covid-19 Pandemic, *European Journal of Theatre and Performance*, 4, pp. 350–385.

Wei, Y. (2023) Invasion as Trespassing Spatial Boundaries: Anti-domestic Violence during the Covid-19 Pandemic, *Performance Research*, 28(3), pp. 107–113.

Willett, C., Willett, J. and Sherman, Y. D. (2012) The Seriously Erotic Politics of Feminist Laughter, *Social Research: An International Quarterly*, 79(1), pp. 217–246.

Wu, J. (2003) From 'Long Yang' and 'Dui Shi' to Tongzhi: Homosexuality in China, *Journal of Gay and Lesbian Psychotherapy*, 7(1–2), pp. 117–143.

Xia, L. (2021) The Silent Noras. *Asian Theatre Journal*, 38(1), pp. 218–244.

Yang, F. and Kavka, M. (2024) Podcasting Women's Pleasure: Feminism and Sexuality in the Sonic Space of China, *Sexualities*, 28(3), 1102–1117.

Yang, X. and Qiu, H. (2024) How Chinese Women Cope with Physical and Psychological Traumas in Gynecological Examinations: A Situational Analysis of Patients' Communicative Accommodations, *International Journal of Communication*, 18, pp. 1677–1697.

Ye, S. (2021) The Drama of Chinese Feminism: Neoliberal Agency, Post-Socialist Coloniality, and Post-Cold War Transnational Feminist Praxis, *Feminist Studies*, 47(3), pp. 783–812.

Yu, Z. L. (2015) *Translating Feminism in China*. Abingdon: Routledge.

Zhao, S. (2016) A Conversation with Ai Xiaoming: When Feminist Activists Encounter Sexual Harassment from Fellow Democrats. *Initium Media*, 7 March, https://theinitium.com/article/20160307-mainland-womansrights.

Zheng, J. (2016) *New Feminism in China: Young Middle-Class Chinese Women in Shanghai*. New York: Springer.

Cambridge Elements

Women Theatre Makers

Elaine Aston
Lancaster University

Elaine Aston is internationally acclaimed for her feminism and theatre research. Her monographs include *Caryl Churchill* (1997); *Feminism and Theatre* (1995); *Feminist Theatre Practice* (1999); *Feminist Views on the English Stage* (2003); and *Restaging Feminisms* (2020). She has served as Senior Editor of Theatre Research International (2010–12) and President of the International Federation for Theatre Research (2019–23).

Melissa Sihra
Trinity College Dublin

Melissa Sihra is Associate Professor in Drama and Theatre Studies at Trinity College Dublin. She is author of *Marina Carr: Pastures of the Unknown* (2018) and editor of *Women in Irish Drama: A Century of Authorship and Representation* (2007). She was President of the Irish Society for Theatre Research (2011–15) and is currently researching a feminist historiography of the Irish playwright and co-founder of the Abbey Theatre, Lady Augusta Gregory.

Advisory Board

Nobuko Anan, *Kansai University, Japan*
Awo Mana Asiedu, *University of Ghana*
Ana Bernstein, *UNIRIO, Brazil*
Elin Diamond, *Rutgers, USA*
Bishnupriya Dutt, *JNU, India*
Penny Farfan, *University of Calgary, Canada*
Lesley Ferris, *Ohio State University, USA*
Lisa FitzPatrick, *University of Ulster, Northern Ireland*
Lynette Goddard, *Royal Holloway, University of London, UK*
Sarah Gorman, *Roehampton University, UK*
Aoife Monks, *Queen Mary, London University, UK*
Kim Solga, *Western University, Canada*
Denise Varney, *University of Melbourne, Australia*

About the Series

This innovative, inclusive series showcases women-identifying theatre makers from around the world. Expansive in chronological and geographical scope, the series encompasses practitioners from the late nineteenth century onwards and addresses a global, comprehensive range of creatives – from playwrights and performers to directors and designers.

Cambridge Elements=

Women Theatre Makers

Elements in the Series

Xin Fengxia and the Transformation of China's Ping Opera
Siyuan Liu

Emma Rice's Feminist Acts of Love
Lisa Peck

Women Making Shakespeare in the Twenty-First Century
Kim Solga

Clean Break Theatre Company
Caoimhe McAvinchey, Sarah Bartley, Deborah Dean and Anne-marie Greene

#WakingTheFeminists and the Data-Driven Revolution in Irish Theatre
Claire Keogh

The Theatre of Louise Lowe
Miriam Haughton

Ellen Terry, Shakespeare, and Suffrage in Australia and New Zealand
Kate Flaherty

Performing Female Intimacy in Japan's Takarazuka Revue
Nobuko Anan

Feminist Imagining in Polish and Ukrainian Theatres
Ewa Bal, Kasia Lech

Caryl Churchill's Eco-Socialist Feminism
Elaine Aston

Lauren Gunderson and Feminist Theatre in the Twenty-First Century
Noelia Hernando-Real

Chinese Feminisms and The Vagina Monologues
Yingjun Wei

A full series listing is available at: www.cambridge.org/EWTM

For EU product safety concerns, contact us at Calle de José Abascal, 56–1°,
28003 Madrid, Spain or eugpsr@cambridge.org.

www.ingramcontent.com/pod-product-compliance
Lightning Source LLC
LaVergne TN
LVHW011857060526
838200LV00054B/4385